A Discovered

Life

Dawn Bennett

A Discovered Life

Halo
PUBLISHING
INTERNATIONAL

H alo
PUBLISHING
INTERNATIONAL

Halo Publishing International
7550 WIH-10 #800, PMB 2069,
San Antonio, TX 78229

First Edition, February 2024
ISBN: 978-1-63765-518-4
Library of Congress Control Number: 2023919958

Halo Publishing International is a self-publishing company that publishes adult fiction and non-fiction, children's literature, self-help, spiritual, and faith-based books. We continually strive to help authors reach their publishing goals and provide many different services that help them do so. We do not publish books that are deemed to be politically, religiously, or socially disrespectful, or books that are sexually provocative, including erotica. Halo reserves the right to refuse publication of any manuscript if it is deemed not to be in line with our principles. Do you have a book idea you would like us to consider publishing? Please visit www.halopublishing.com for more information.

The abandoned child in me thanks everyone who tried to love her. She remembers her love for Chuck Bennett, who wanted to be her playmate for forty-five happy years of marriage.

Contents

Preface

Dawn, age four: "Momma and Daddy are selling our house because Daddy is going to the Navy. Daddy sure gets muddy working down in our basement because Momma said he has to make a real basement. She says they can sell the house for more money after he fixes it. They don't let me go down there and get muddy."

Dawn, age five: "We have to live with Aunt Gee now because Daddy and Uncle Jack left for the Navy. Aunt Gee owns this whole apartment house with four people who pay her their rent. I met Herman and Grace. They are nice, and so is Eleanor. Eleanor draws pictures for the newspaper. Momma showed me a picture. It was a pretty lady in a fancy dress."

Dawn, age five and a half: "There are no children here to play with. Aunt Gee found one little girl, and we played dolls, but Momma said I can't play with her anymore. Momma said that girl stole the special doll clothes that Grandma Moore made for me. Both the moms argued. The girl's mom said I gave the other girl the doll clothes, and now she doesn't want her to play with me."

"I get to take dancing lessons because there will be some other girls. I went to the dance lessons, but I forgot to get off the bus at the right place. I got lost. A nice man helped me, but Momma said I should not have trusted a strange man."

Dawn, age six: "We finally moved to Norfolk, where Daddy's Navy is. There are some children here, but they are all boys. I don't like boys because they want to put ice down my shirt. One boy chased me with a bug. I don't like bugs, either. I have to go to school now.

As I walked up to the school, I practiced saying my ABCs. I kept saying the first ones, but I couldn't remember the one after *E*. I was worried that I am dumb, but Momma says it's okay; the school will teach me."

Dawn, age six and a half: "I met a girl at the playground, and she was teaching me how to do a flip on the monkey bars. I did it right, but I forgot to keep my hands on the bar. Momma got mad because she thinks my nose might be broken from falling."

Dawn, age seven: "We came to Panama on a big Navy ship with guns. Navy guys were out on the deck, and one offered me a candy bar. I had to throw up, and the man was upset. He said other people were on deck because they were seasick. Momma says that's what I had.

I like Panama. Daddy took us way far away where the grass huts were. He told us about coconut trees and asked if I wanted him to climb up and get a coconut so I could drink the juice. I said no because I might not like that juice."

Dawn, age seven and a half: "The principal wants to put me back in first grade because I don't read very well. Momma is going to teach me phonics and says she will catch me up. That principal is my second-grade teacher. She had to tend to an emergency when a boy broke off a pencil in his ear. She always puts our work on the board before she leaves, and everybody else does it. I fussed at her and told her I could not read the assignment. She was mad at me. I hope Mom can catch me up."

Dawn, third grade: "I am back in Roanoke, and I am smarter than my whole class. I can write in cursive, but the rest of the class hasn't learned that yet. I thought I could just relax and maybe do some drawing while they practice writing. My teacher made me mad. I have to practice with the class. They do this weird thing about shaping the letters. The teacher always knows I add on curves to the letters' endings. You are supposed to start and end with curves. My letters look okay, but she says they aren't good enough. This way of writing is called the Locker method."

Dawn, fourth through sixth grades: "I go to church and school, and there are some children there. I am different from the others because I can't do some things. I never did any kickball or baseball. I had rheumatic fever before and had to lie quietly on a blanket, or I might die. Mrs. Price, my sixth-grade teacher, really likes me, and she wants me to do sports like the other children. Last week, she yelled and cheered for me so much that I finally hit the baseball. David caught it really quick, and it was still an out, but everyone was really surprised I hit it.

My baby brother is growing up, and we moved from the rented house that Uncle Howard got for us, to the new house we bought. Momma said buying the new house was so expensive that she could only afford new pajamas for my birthday. She sat me on her knee and said, 'My little girl.' I wasn't really a little girl anymore, but I was glad my family was happy."

Dawn, seventh grade and age thirteen: "Mostly, I went to church alone, and I learned in school. Now I am in junior high school, and they do initiation with beginning students. Mom was upset when I came home with lipstick writing on my face. I liked it! The older kids did it to me, and I said okay.

We live in a new neighborhood where Daddy helped Uncle Howard build and fix the houses. Momma says that's the only way we could get a house like this. Daddy left the Navy, and he is going to be a policeman. He always says he is, a 'jack-of-all-trades and master of none.' I think he's good at a lot of stuff.

I have been so confused about being okay because Momma and the church say two different things. I need to be saved at church, but Momma says I could do better if I just tried hard. I had a bad experience last week, and I feel really bad. I cried hard. I went to a revival, and at the end of the service, I decided to go down the aisle and confess my sins like you are supposed to do when you are ready. I wasn't sure exactly what my sins were, but I was sorry for any bad stuff I had done, and I told God that. Teachers at church told me that would be okay.

When I got to the front of the church, a woman came up to me and asked if I had been saved. I said I wasn't sure. She seemed really angry and asked me two more times. She said that I would know if I was saved, and she was getting more upset, so I said I was saved. Since I still am not sure I am saved, I guess I lied. I never want to lie. Daddy told me that was one of the worst things you could do.

I feel like crying again. I don't understand what to do, and I hate to tell anyone because I am embarrassed. I feel awful about lying."

Chapter 1

No Treasure Map for My Path

"What do you want to be when you grow up?"

"A psychiatrist," I replied, my youthful voice ringing out with spontaneity and conviction. I liked that question. It assumes that I will be something and that I have a choice.

Mom laughed. "You have to get a college degree, and that takes four years. Next, you have to get a medical degree and then specialize. That probably takes about six more years."

I may have given up all dreams at that time.

Here's my story.

Maybe we are dropped into families at random. Why would we think they should love us? Some of my friends believe in reincarnation and think we pick our families before we arrive here. Each lifetime is supposed to be a different learning experience. Their belief is stronger than mine, so I won't argue that point. Plus, it's an interesting possibility.

Family history often repeats itself. I inherited my parents' difficulties and disappointments and did not feel much love from them. Mom's family had very little love to give anyone. Her father was the school janitor and her mom had to raise his first four children while raising their next four on his income alone. They were from a simple family farm in rural Virginia.

Mom was the second of her mother's biological children and the oldest girl. This role made her very responsible. Fortunately, my dad rescued her eighteen years later. He was a wonderful man and loved her dearly. He was the second-oldest boy and welcomed quitting school in eighth grade to become the man of the family when his own father was disabled at work in a railroad accident.

Mom and Dad's marriage looked like a success. What a disappointment to Mom that Dad became an alcoholic for the first fifteen years of my life. Turned out, she needed his love in order to love me.

Both of them were high school dropouts. And when the depression hit our country near the time of my birth, it was a difficult period for everyone. My father's lack of work and income affected my parents' happiness. I don't know all the details because I wasn't there, but they revealed small facts from time to time. I listened and put together an impression of two loving adults failing in their best efforts, when they had a child to care for. Mom was the responsible person, and she had no fun. She certainly was not happy.

I needed to learn to love myself in order to be happy. This has been real work during my entire lifetime since history repeats itself. I have heard many teach what they need to learn and have arrived at self-love after a long journey of knowing myself, and evaluating my time spent here on the planet. I do not mean I love that egocentric, artificial person with the false smile; the one who was taught to please others. Rather, I began to love myself as a self-evaluating, self-respecting, mostly honest version of who I came to be.

My church taught me that God loves me, so I needed to be a good girl. I thought of this in the same way as I did Santa at Christmastime, sometimes uncertain whether I was being a good girl. Would God love me if I wasn't?

I was sent to church and some of the people there seemed to like me, but they did not even know me. It seemed as if most of the teachers were nice women, and at vacation Bible school we got free candy. I liked that, as well as some of the stories they told about a loving Jesus, so I kept going to church. Momma liked me to go to Bible school, and the teachers seemed to like me a lot.

As I grew older, people told me how Jesus was so different and had lived a long time ago. The teachers told me He was God's only son, and He liked everybody, just as God did. When things were bad at home, I tried to remember God and Jesus loved me. I kept learning more and more about how good girls were supposed to act, and I usually tried hard to do those things. My whole life I had to learn which things were bad, sinful, or wrong to do, though not everyone agreed. Figuring out my own rules was sometimes difficult.

Granma Moore, Dad's mom, was the first person who really knew me and seemed to love me. She made special clothes for my doll. She showed me how to make a row of paper dolls out of a folded newspaper and how to crochet. I loved her.

Next, there was Mabel, the lady who lived with us when Daddy went to the Navy in Norfolk, Virginia. She listened to me and tried to help when she could. Once, when I didn't eat all the food on my plate at dinner, she showed me how to eat ham on a biscuit so I would not get in trouble for not finishing.

Mrs. Hart was the third one I remember loving me and the other children. She took our whole church class to an amusement park and, for no reason, bought me a soda out of her own money. I was too surprised to know if I loved her. I had learned soda was not good for little girls, so buying me a soda went against the grown-up rules. That was confusing.

All three of these special women taught me something about love as a child. They noticed me, paid attention to me, and showed caring behavior. I did not get much of that in my family since I lived in an adults-only environment for my first six years. The message that I was a bother was frequently communicated in various ways until I became more mature. I could never go back to early childhood, but I recognized that adult approval meant much more to me as I evolved into others' preferences.

There seemed to be no map for my life as I began to go to school. I never dreamed of being anyone whom people might admire. I wasn't very smart, and I had no friends. I had no outstanding talents and received little recognition for any small successes.

My family seemed to live paycheck to paycheck and had little expectation of having different choices in life. Dad, with an eighth-grade education, became a policeman, and Mom had various jobs that allowed my family of two parents and two children to function better than many of our neighbors.

As I continue to review my life, I never imagined I would be the first college graduate in our family, or anything else that was exceptional. I never dreamed I could be a respected professional, a family therapist. I had never heard about specializing in family therapy until I went to graduate school, and I never ever imagined going to college until my senior year in high school. Becoming a psychiatrist was a desire I recognized, but was hidden way down in my heart; I had given up on most all my dreams when I was younger.

On my life journey, I almost missed several of the treasures that marked my way. For instance, my mom taught me to have few expectations, and I mistakenly translated that as I wasn't deserving of much. If I had recognized her message might mean, "Wait patiently, and choose the good stuff," I would have felt better emotionally. Because her message was "I had a life so much worse than yours," I misunderstood what she was trying to tell me. It was difficult to complain to her. Once, she had told me that as a child, she only got fruit, raisins, and a little candy for Christmas if, she was really good.

Reducing my expectations caused me to be a rather numb child. From time to time I did complain, but there was never much benefit to that; so I began to gradually expect less and less. I focused on how going to church would make me a good girl, and then I would be happy, or so I was told. I am uncertain if I ever felt satisfied or comfortable as a child. Sometimes, I was anxious and I internalized my feelings.

This was true until I had success as a speaker. I learned public speaking in Sunday-night classes at the Baptist Training Union; I was forced to attend. I figured I might as well learn to better speak positively to others, and soon I became a favorite of teachers and my parents' adult friends.

I did not trust myself as I grew older, constantly wanting and needing approval. I behaved well usually, but was uncertain about caring relationships. Maybe I couldn't love others because I felt so little love myself. I looked for female friendships and had little success.

I was in the eighth grade before a teacher told me that she wanted me to become Lynda's friend. She may have noticed that I had no friends, but she never mentioned it. Lynda and I were friends all the way through high school. The eighth-grade teacher discovered that Lynda and I liked art so, we drew pictures each month for one of the blackboards. It was fun and one of my first memories of friendship.

One day, I found a picture of me in our family album. I was shocked. This small five-year-old had her hands on her hips and her legs spread apart. Her stance was strong, and the expression on her face was different from any I had ever seen. Was this really me? How had I missed this picture?

I began to think of who that little girl seemed to be. Slowly, I came to understand why I had taken so long to rebel, and why my rebellion fluctuated so much. You can lose love when you rebel, and I didn't have enough love to waste. Living in an all-adult world made me feel criticized which I thought was unfair. I internally celebrated that defiant little girl inside me; she deserved better treatment. Eventually, she became an internal guide for my self-esteem.

My irritation and anger came from believing things should be different. That small girl thought she knew what she wanted, but the growing girl became uncertain. I never wanted to know my mom had so little to appreciate and enjoy in her life, but that explains my training. She told about her childhood so that I might appreciate my better life.

There is not much I remember enjoying during my childhood. My first memory is about my being really, really bad—Mom said I mooned the babysitter. Katie, my favorite babysitter, came by with her boyfriend Phil, and wanted to take me for a ride in his new truck. I usually liked that though playing outside with other children was always my favorite. I hardly ever got to do that. So, Mom says, I turned my butt to Katie and dropped my panties. I don't really remember that. How did I learn to do that? I am sure I had never seen that behavior before. In any event, my mother took me right in the house and spanked me hard.

I must have learned then that I was a bad girl. I did not have many opportunities to play with other children after that event. My parents sold our home in the midst of the depression. Daddy was going to the Navy, and Mom and

I would live with Aunt Gee. There were no other good choices for them because there was little money from jobs.

Momma said I got a bunny and a kitty one Christmas. I can't believe that! I would have considered that being spoiled, and that it did not happen unless Daddy had been drinking a lot. Mom did say Dad had promised he wouldn't let me keep the bunny, that he would take it back after the holidays and I would be left with just the kitty. That's what I remember happened, but I did not keep the kitty very long, either. Mom said we did not need animals to feed and take care of. She was a farm girl; the chickens and cow were worth taking care of and feeding, but not house animals that just caused a mess and cost money to feed.

Mainly, I remember the times after Daddy went away to the war, when we lived with Aunt Gee. Momma said all the adults did not want to be bothered by me. There were no other children and I couldn't figure out what "bothering" was. Sometimes it was noise, sometimes it was interrupting, and sometimes it was "playing too hard in the house.". The rules kept changing. If I could just be good enough, I was sure I would get some love.

I had only one playmate at Aunt Gee's, in the beginning; the little girl with whom I shared the doll clothes Gramma Moore had made. Since she had taken them, and told her mom I gave them to her, my mom got very angry.

The doll clothes were special, and the little girl had stolen them. I was sad that I never had any playmates after that.

Sometimes, my mom and aunt took me to funny movies. I liked that. I helped set the table before meals and I listened to some shows on the radio. I liked to draw and I was allowed to use the phone pad to write on. Occasionally, when I was very upset, they bought me colored crayons with which to draw. After a while, I was allowed to have some paper dolls and learned to draw new clothes on them and color them.

I was also sent to dance class sometimes. There were other girls there, and I learned to dance as they did. We all did the same things but usually, there were no children my age in the classes.

I grew up to be a better girl because I learned to behave better. And I helped with my brother. He was born when I was six years old and everyone liked him.

The next year, I almost died; I was about seven years old. I had rheumatic fever and had to lie quietly on a blanket all summer. I did not get to play very much until we moved to Panama.

While we lived in the military housing in Norfolk, I was invited to spend the night with one girl and hoped we would be friends. During that night, she said she wanted to do something she liked; her big sister had taught her this thing. I said okay, and she did something on my girl parts that sort of tickled. She wanted me to do that to her, but I said no.

When I went home, I told Mom about it. She was really angry and we had to go to the girl's house to tell her mom. The moms were really unhappy, and I knew I couldn't be friends with this girl either.

It seemed as if I could never have girlfriends. All the children who visited us were boys. Mom's friends all had boys and I thought they were awful. They tried to put bugs down my shirt. They liked to tease me, just like Uncle Jack, Aunt Gee's husband.

Next, we moved to Panama to be with Daddy and everybody was happier. There was a girl named Patsy downstairs from us, and the moms wanted us to be friends! Patsy warned me about the children from Panama on our school bus. They had different hair from us, and she said not to be afraid if they wanted to touch mine. I was sorry they never asked to touch my hair. I would have liked that.

All the rest of my childhood I continued to try and be a good girl. I went to church by myself to learn to love others better. Momma said that's what they did at church, but she had to stay home with my baby brother.

The rest of my story can be summed up by saying I did what was expected of me, most of the time, and most adults liked me very much. Adults liking me felt almost like love. I liked all the women church leaders and schoolteachers. They smiled a lot, and they paid attention to me.

Sometimes, I did really good things, and they noticed. Mrs. McDonald, one of my schoolteachers, told me my design in art was so good she was mailing it to the linoleum company; they sometimes paid for designs. I won the library's poster contest with my picture of a "book worm" crawling out of the page. Mom said the judges decided I must have had help because it was "too good for a child to do alone." That time, she took up for me, but I still didn't win because the judges thought she helped me.

In third grade, Mrs. Elliot picked me to be the actress in the play about teddy bears, and she didn't even like poor kids like me. The buses from the projects brought kids like me into the richest school in town, near where she lived. When I couldn't tie the bow on the teddy correctly, she got upset and picked another girl to be the actress.

In fifth grade, we rented a house and I was able to go to another school. I had never attended a school that had sports, where children chose teams for kickball and baseball. No one wanted me on their team, but Mrs. Elliott liked me. One day, she cheered so hard for me that I hit the baseball. I was so surprised I forgot to run; Billy caught the ball, so I was out anyway.

Once, in seventh grade, I made lots of As. And in ninth, I made the honor roll one time. Then studying got harder and I didn't try as much.

Tenth and eleventh grades' new subjects were harder and I felt less confident. This only changed, slightly, my senior year in high school. I was sitting next to Norris Munson in homeroom, and she heard me say I wasn't going to college.

She said, "Why aren't you going to college? You are smart enough. You should go."

I took this message home to Mom and Dad. Mom said I probably only wanted to attend college to have fun and find a good husband. Dad said I should go to college if I really wanted to go for the right reasons.

Dad worked out a plan to take me to Radford College, a community college nearest to us. With his eighth-grade education, having dropped out of school to help his family by getting a job, he apparently valued education for me. I was quiet and shocked when we walked onto the campus, and he asked a student where the president's office was. He led us directly to that office where my father asked to speak to the president.

The flustered secretary seemed as confused as I felt before the president walked out and asked how he could help us. Dad made it clear that he could not afford the tuition and wondered about work programs. By the time we left that office, I was registered for a work scholarship in the dining room, waiting tables. If I had had more confidence my senior year, I wonder what other possibilities I could have seriously considered.

Norris Munson was our best actress at Jefferson High. She invited me to go to theater tryouts at a local place. She did not get a callback, but I did. I had never focused on this particular talent of mine, even though I had won the leading role in the ninth-grade play and was said to be "inspirational" by a teacher at church. My high school performance was as the sex bomb in a one-act play. I had role diversity and some talent.

My parents always worked and never saw any of my performances. When they heard about my callback, Mom said, "We don't have a way for you to get back and forth for rehearsals because we don't have a car." That was the end of even more ideas for my future.

College offered my first independence from home. After one year at Radford, I followed my mom's practical thinking. I was having a good time, but did not think I was learning anything that would help me get a job. Mom had a friend with a good job in the telephone company; she promised me a job. So, I departed for my final summer vacation. I was becoming a responsible adult, and my friends from college who lived nearby in Washington, DC, welcomed me to visit.

What an amazing phone call I received from home that was to change my entire life! Mom was so excited. Aunt Ida, Dad's sister; Uncle Howard; our minister and his wife, had worked with Mom and Dad to enroll me in Baylor University in Texas. When Mom explained how she had to write my autobiography for me to meet the time constraints, I angrily hung up the phone. How dare she pretend to be me! I had never been so angry with her. I couldn't imagine going all the way to Texas and being known as what she had described me to be.

My college friends tried to reason with me by saying that going to a university for a degree was such a good opportunity. I had been dating a friend of theirs, Dayton. We had gone to play the slots in New Jersey, ridden the local waterways in his motorboat, and had lots of fun. Dayton also encouraged me to go to Baylor, and he promised that if I was unhappy after six weeks, he would come to rescue me in his new Edsel.

All the persuasion of my peers convinced me to at least give more college life a chance. None of them had been offered the chance for advanced education, and all were going to be starting new lives together around DC. I could not afford to live on my own yet.

Dayton called to check on me after six weeks, and I was mostly satisfied with my dormitory life on campus. These Texas guys with cowboy hats, who were walking the campus, were a strange new variety for me; the girls in the dorm were very feminine and attractive; and the Christian values already instilled in most of them matched mine. After graduation three years later, I was glad I had gone to Baylor. Getting an art major was very gratifying, and I imagined I could get a teaching job very easily as an English double major with some skills for teaching elementary school.

In the fall of 1960, I made my first totally independent decision. I had graduated from Baylor University, a Baptist college, but without credentials for a teaching position in Virginia. I would marry in June of 1961, but I didn't know it because I had not yet met my intended. This was the happy part; the sad parts came later.

I had met Chuck before, when several of my friends and I ran into him and a group of his friends at the amusement park. That time, we greeted each other and kept going. He looked just like one of the gang he was with. I noticed he was attractive as I consciously ticked off all his positive points, which included his dark, curly hair and nice body. I noticed the cigarettes rolled up in his sleeves, to show off his muscles. I also smoked, but he was seemingly proud of his smoking habit and his muscles. He resembled the "toughs" in popular movies. That was not my value system, and I dismissed him as a candidate for my further interest.

When I met him later at Shoney's, a fast-food hangout, I was impressed. There was a popular style of collegiate sweaters that he was wearing, and he also had that trendy, neat crew-cut hairstyle. My friend Sandy and I sat and talked with him for a while. He had transferred from Syracuse University to Roanoke College as a math major. He had one more year to go because he'd lost credits in the transfer.

I was about to begin my career as a public schoolteacher in the county, and felt independent and confident as a graduate of Baylor University. Though I was living with my parents, I felt mature and self-sufficient. I seemed several steps ahead of Chuck, but he had good potential. I never thought of him as a potential date, but when he spoke of "breaking up with Betty," his fiancée, I felt aligned with his emotional pain.

Once again, I was impressed. He seemed to be taking the breakup well, as he laughed about needing to spend the money from their joint savings account. I was impressed that they *had* a joint savings account.

When Sandy called to say she had a date with Chuck, I was pleased for her. She wanted me to double-date with an Army friend of his that Saturday night; they were going to a dance club we liked. I was reluctant until I thought of my new potential identity as an old-maid schoolteacher. Dating in Roanoke and working in the county might be difficult while living at home. So, I agreed to go.

The guys picked me up and my date was attractive. Chuck pointed out that he had on civilian clothes, but was wearing army boots. We agreed this was not good for dancing, but my date said he was not a dancer anyway. That feeling of dread began to overtake me again.

During the course of the evening, I put on some lipstick. I had a tissue in my hand and asked in a humorous way if anyone wanted to blot my lipstick for me. I was totally shocked when Chuck offered. I was so shocked in fact, I can't remember the actual event. As predicted, the evening was a total loss. Sandy and Chuck left my date and me in the booth alone for most of the evening; I don't remember any conversation in particular. I am certain I was not my most congenial self.

A few days later, Chuck called to ask me out on a date. I was suspicious and questioned him about Sandy's knowing he was asking me out. He said he had not told her, but it was okay if I wanted to. I called Sandy, and she said they were just friends; he was not her type. She further stated that he was such a "straight arrow" that if he kissed a girl, he probably planned to marry her. I called Chuck back and agreed to go out to a downtown bar where we could get acquainted and talk.

I would never have thought of the place we were going since I only drank when I went dancing. It seemed sophisticated to me. He asked me what to order and I had no clue. I said I did not like beer, and he suggested we try Champale. I had never heard of this but I liked the lighter taste, and we each had two during our long evening.

Conversation was easy, and Chuck explained "Bennett's religion." I was impressed with his practical, common-sense view of morality. He had written a paper called "The Problem of Evil" as a college thesis, in which he questioned many familiar positions about life and religion.

Since I had been reluctant to attend Baylor in the beginning of my college education, and I was tired of being the Baptist model of a good girl before college, I was very attracted to Chuck's ease with our conversation. His former fiancée, Betty, had been a Catholic girl who finally broke it off with him over some of their religious differences. I briefly wondered about him being on the rebound, but he seemed to have no regrets about the end of their engagement.

When we arrived at my house at the end of the evening, I watched Chuck put his glasses over the sun visor. I sat very still, waiting to see if he was the straight arrow Sandy had predicted. When he leaned over and kissed me passionately, I was almost breathless, but quickly thought of being the one to slow things down. I had so *very* much practice with this slowing-down tactic, and I wondered where Chuck had practiced kissing. I thought of Sandy's comment and that he might want to marry me. Briefly delighted, I was now in conflict. Who was this guy?

There was a second and a third date before Steve called. What an unexpected dilemma. Steve was a really attractive guy I had dated at home over my last summer break. I would normally have been glad to see him again, but

I felt torn about accepting his invitation. I told him in a meaningful way that I had met someone, and we were in a committed relationship. I felt manipulative because I knew it was a small lie, or an unestablished fact at the very least. Thankfully, Chuck said, "Then we are," after I shared what I had told Steve. I received the reassurance I needed that we were both equally attracted and serious.

The first day we planned for Chuck to meet my mom, a strange event intervened. Chuck was in chemistry lab that day. As we were talking, I noticed the fabric of the pants he was wearing; some parts looked threadbare. I wanted him to make a good impression, and he looked okay otherwise. As I was preoccupied and continued to stare at the fabric of his pants, I thought my eyes were deceiving me. I called Chuck's attention to his pants as we both witnessed more threads disappear. He was alarmed His pants were being eaten away by acid in the air of the chemistry lab! We left quickly so that his first meeting with my mom would not be with him half naked.

Before I introduced Chuck to my mother, I needed some insurance she would approve of him. Mother had previously shown racial prejudice in several ways. I decided I would tell her that Chuck was very dark-skinned. I told her that I had not asked about his family's origins, but they might be "Mexican or something." It worked. Mom said she liked him and did not think he was a problem regarding his family or his heritage.

Dad met Chuck much later than Mom since he worked alternate shifts and wasn't around as often. That event also occurred with unusual circumstances. When Chuck approached my house late one evening, my dad was yelling at my mom. Chuck later told me that Dad was in his undershirt, and his gun was still strapped to his hip. My mom had just arrived home after a visit with her sisters in San Diego, where she had become a platinum blonde. Dad did not recognize her at the airport and was embarrassed since he was in his police uniform. He was yelling about her new look as Chuck approached the door.

Mom had thought Dad would be pleased by her new look. That evening when Chuck bravely knocked on the door, he was hoping I would greet him. It probably took some time before Chuck realized my father, the policeman, was actually quite gentle.

Chuck and I dated through September and October, and on my birthday in November, he asked me to marry him. Since he could not afford to buy me an engagement ring, I was tempted to buy my own; however, we were able to work out a plan. He would take part of his weekly family allowance as a college student to make regular payments at the jeweler store, and I would assist with money for our social activities.

Dad was very helpful at this point. He had interrupted a robbery at a jewelry store during his police duty so, in appreciation, the jewelry store's owner accepted Chuck's financial guarantee to continue payments. Now, I would receive a small diamond ring for my birthday. I was so pleased to show off my ring, even though it was very small.

During the half year of our engagement, there was little money for dates. Mom found a couple from our church who square-danced, and we took lessons. I liked to dance and it was so inexpensive. It seemed a poor substitute for the beach-boogie music and dancing I liked, but couples at square dancing were married and usually into church. We would have that in common.

Bridge was a game Chuck liked, so I began to learn to play. It was free. We also had one couple with whom we could spend time. Sarah and Dickie were going to marry in June. We played games and, very occasionally, could afford bowling with them.

Chuck had to study frequently and I had papers to grade. He helped me design short-answer tests for less paper-work. I always had to include a "Kay question." Kay was my only student who made straight As, and I thought it was important to challenge her. My other students were less focused on grades, but I wanted my testing to be fair for the entire class. I only included one Kay question per test. She usually got a 95 on her tests because she missed only that one question.

I took educating my class very seriously and noticed most of the children in this farming community were uncomplicated. They were direct, honest, and had lower expectations. Their acceptance gave me confidence as the new "city girl." I learned that many of the teachers were not credentialed. They taught by special arrangement with the state since there was a shortage of trained teachers in the region, and the salaries were low.

Recognizing I had this job because I would accept the lower salary and use the year to complete my own credentials, I was relatively comfortable and I enjoyed the children. I enjoyed them so much, in fact, that I made a dumb plan. Looking back, I realize I almost ended my career before it began.

I wanted to give the children a Christmas party, so I had them bring permission slips if they could go. There were so few with permission that Chuck and I decided to drive them to my house in Roanoke for the party. We borrowed the pastor's larger station wagon and all went well until the return trip. It had snowed and Chuck missed the turn on one country road. We did not go into the ditch, fortunately, but when we got out to assess our situation, I could see the station wagon had at least one wheel off the road.

I told the children to sit very still and possibly hold hands for balance, if needed. I told Chuck to go up the road to the country store, which was visible from our location. I was certain several guys hovering around the potbellied stove in the store would come to push the wagon back onto the road. As I predicted, all of this happened.

To this very day I realize how fraught with problems this scenario was. I was able to keep the events secret because of the permission slips and with the children's appreciation of our "adventure." I learned from this risky, frightening situation.

From our engagement in November to our wedding in June, Chuck and I had little privacy. Much of our dating time was spent in parked cars for limited privacy. Both Chuck and I lived at home with our families, and our favorite song became "Alone at Last." It is a beautiful melody and represented our desire for intimacy. Daddy, as my policeman father, kept asking me where the good parking spots were. We had regular conversation about neither Chuck nor I knowing any private parking spots.

One night, we were discovered by a random police car. We beat them out of that secluded area, motivated by our fear and rapid response. As it became obvious how careful we needed to be, we discovered our best spot was on the church grounds at night. It was nearby, and the area did not seem to attract any attention.

Youthful passion was a huge problem for us. We were constantly aroused and feared pregnancy. Chuck studied at my house most nights and because Mom loved him so much, he could leave the coffeepot on and fall asleep until morning. Those things are not easily forgiven in our home. Neither of my parents knew that Chuck sometimes came into my downstairs room for a good-night kiss. My parents slept upstairs. We practiced marvelous self-control until one of my college friends, Gail, invited us to her wedding that May.

We arranged to stay at Cousin Eddie's in Alexandria in order to attend the wedding. We had separate rooms. There was a champagne fountain at the wedding, and we both had a wonderful time. After we returned to Eddie's house, we gave them a review of the wedding events before going upstairs to change out of our wedding finery. Both of us got totally out of control when we went upstairs and I gave no thought to the possibility of being discovered. Chuck totally distracted me when he lifted me off the floor to be closer and more intimate. The fear of pregnancy was very real, but we only had little more than a month before our honeymoon.

We wanted to comply with our parents' limits and expectations since we expected to have Chuck graduate with his full degree and an excellent job. When he had shared that we would not wait until graduation to be married, his parents were concerned. This was the test I had demanded of him. Facing his parents was his job, alone.

He had to take responsibility with his parents for our marriage in June. I had offered to go live with Aunt Gee in San Francisco until we could marry. The tension was getting to me, but Chuck was afraid that much separation would be too much for our relationship. He agreed to face his parents' disapproval.

They offered us the car he was driving, or a year's college tuition. I chose the tuition because I knew I could not support his college expenses on my limited teaching salary while also paying for household expenses.

Since I had not yet qualified for Virginia's state teaching credential after I graduated from Baylor, I was on a limited-salary arrangement awaiting certification. I had to complete a couple of courses, which I was taking by correspondence. I would receive a large check and my teaching certificate if I completed everything by June. I knew my salary would be better the next year. I was confident I could meet the requirements since I was so motivated.

A job in the distant, poor farming community was all that I could get. It was forty-five minutes out of town, and I did not drive. I had to carpool with three other teachers, but felt lucky to have a teaching job. Chuck and I could not begin our married life with any dark clouds hanging over us. We felt we would have many years ahead when we could enjoy everything we were missing. Passionate love, hope, and promises kept us going each day. Chuck was my ultimate treasure along the map of my future life.

I should have known that from the first personal encounter when he shared his own life goals and values.

Life was easier for me since Mom was impressed with my fiancé. She had always worried about my finding a good man. Dad was impressed that Chuck went to church with me. The entire church was impressed with their "favorite daughter," who had just completed her degree at a large, respected Baptist university.

The pastor talked to Chuck about joining the church and later told me, "If Chuck had known you had to be baptized to join the church, he would never have done it."

I responded, "You might want to start fresh in your marriage."

The night Chuck was immersed for baptism, I was sitting in the pew next to Auntie Irene. Irene almost swallowed her tongue when she gulped down the shock of seeing our small minister, Reverend Neeley, dunk Chuck under the water in the baptismal pool. She whispered to me, "He's going to drown. He's going to drop him."

That had never occurred to me, and I wonder now what the entire Bennett family thought of Chuck following me into strong alliance with a church. They saw church attendance as social and moral aspects of life. I was to later learn they were professed atheists. Mom Bennett was an animal lover and said if Christians didn't believe animals went to heaven, she didn't plan to go either.

The stupor cast over me by the visions of our perfect future life, allowed me to accept the invitation; Chuck and I were asked to lead the four-year-old class at church. This group was gentle and had perfect innocence; we were enchanted by the appearance of the children, all washed, brushed, dressed up, and present for Sunday school. Maybe this was suggestive of our future.

Chapter 2

Discovering Us

Looking back, I can see some greater benefit to teaching the four-year-olds since Chuck and I did not attend adult class at the Baptist church. At Baylor, I could keep my disbelief to a minimum since Religion 101 was a required course and an easy class in which to get an A. That grade motivated me to ignore other issues. Neither Chuck nor I would remain faithful to the church after marriage, as we differed from these Baptist adults.

We had to disagree with the pastor's wife when we finally began to attend with the adults. She made us aware we needed to bring others from foreign countries into our faith. Chuck and I did not think this was a reasonable expectation, even though she said there were lots of missionaries to help. Chuck and I discussed the unfairness of expecting people in other countries to adapt to our beliefs. Blindfolded bliss in our new marriage kept us unaware in the beginning, but Baptist adults asked us to embrace some ideas we could not share.

One of my first rebellions was this alliance against my former beliefs after marrying a loving mate. I could risk family rejection for the first time, because of this trust-worthy alliance. I did not consciously realize I needed a rebellion, since family love always seemed available through joint beliefs and values. I appear to have even accepted joint beliefs unconsciously in most of my past relationships.

The church first told me God loved me, but I did not feel that love within my churchgoing family in everyday life. Later, I was told Jesus loved me. After hearing some of the stories about Jesus, I began to believe that He might. Afterall, I had some wonderful Sunday school teachers and youth leaders who seemed loving. Still, I felt a need to hide from a vengeful, punishing God that I had encountered in the Old Testament. A loving Jesus but not God remains a contradiction I arrived to in my consciousness one day. I needed to find the loving God of the Bible, and I had some difficulty doing that when I read the stories of the Old Testament.

Working with the children's innocence and the adults' judgmental style brought my conflicts into sharp contrast. Chuck and I planned to have children one day; therefore, I thought we might need some practice living the values we were developing within our own family. We began to think of Chuck's Methodist history, but I did not trust his leadership in matters of faith. I had been the leader.

I had always made extra money as a neighborhood babysitter. Since Chuck and I were so talented together in the church class, I decided we could do babysitting together too. My first disappointment seemed significant. Chuck enjoyed playing with the children. I was eager for them to go to bed on time and behave well.

One evening, we babysat three children in a family whose eldest child was about five years old and a charming redhead. He grabbed Chuck's attention while I fought for the correct curfew. I was getting angry and losing my cool. When this child got out of bed for the third time, I had had it. Chuck shamed me by graciously accepting the precious handmade valentine that child later brought us; I felt slightly guilty for losing my patience.

This is not the picture I want to present to my readers, but on some level, I was aware I was not totally willing to be a loving mom. Babysitting was a part-time job and, for me, a well-paid one. Being a loving mom would be a fulltime one and not easy.

I began to worry Chuck might be an overly indulgent father. I was not consciously exploring my possible unwillingness to have children; however, I was close every time my future mother-in-law made an issue of our having a baby.

Chuck had one more year of school to complete after we were married. I was not eager to go from adult responsibilities to full-family responsibilities. My mom's enjoyment of a couple's life was fully visible to me now. Dad did not drink anymore, and they had some time and money for leisure. I wanted some of that adult enjoyment.

Dad went to AA first, then he became a deacon in the church. Life was good for my parents for the first time. Somewhere deeply embedded in their issues was the model of what I wanted. I was tired of the repression of sexuality during the period of time Chuck and I were engaged. I knew we wanted to be a couple and to enjoy the compatibility of our union. We were each other's best friend because we had explored our beliefs and plans for future career goals. We weren't typical young people, but hardworking, serious, barely adult churchgoers.

Our best friends, Sarah and Dickie, were similar, but did not go to church. Sarah wanted to be a gym teacher since she loved sports. Dickie was going into the Marines first, and I discussed with Chuck how this lifestyle with travel and adventure might be ideal. He let me know he was 4-F and would never be accepted into the armed forces because of his severe hip injury from a car accident in high school. He also persuaded me that I would not like military life since he could be sent anywhere by military command, and we would not have a choice. He could even get an unaccompanied tour of duty. I was not aware of any of these relevant facts, but all young men at this time had to consider them.

Later, I was delighted to become a pacifist; Chuck and I would discuss whether we would have fled to Canada if he were draft eligible. Before the war in Vietnam, lots of our friends liked the ideas of free love and living in communes. Exploring popular ideas such as these, in these speculative ways, allowed us to realize our values were very similar. We both liked commune living up to the point of desiring other sexual partners. It was very important to me we share this limit about marital fidelity. I took "til death do us part" very seriously.

My friend Sarah had heard about birth control pills during her last year of college, but I did not know about *any* birth control. Before we married, I contacted a doctor and learned about this wonderful insurance against pregnancy. Many young women shared tales of the failure of birth control. I was alert to these consequences and took full responsibility.

When we had to use condoms until the pills began to work; Chuck had a sad tale to tell. The clerk at our local store dismissed Chuck's complaint about the condom that broke. "You were probably so eager you punched a hole in it" was not a compassionate response to our problem. We were eager for the sexual release marriage would bring, but needed to trust birth control methods.

Mother had planned our wedding at the Baptist church. I did not argue because I had no expectations for my own wedding. I had never seen a *Brides* magazine or been to a bridal shower. I had no idea about the expected gifts. Mom however, was on top of each issue and I floated along for the first time in my life. Mom seemed to truly love me. She wanted me to have a beautiful wedding.

When we went to the bridal show at the local department store, she selected the most expensive gown for me. I broke down in tears during the fitting. I said, "I don't deserve this." I had never experienced that kind of an emotional high around my mom before. I had never felt as if I deserved very much beyond necessities.

When I was sent to the photographers' studio for my bridal portrait, I was surprised how large it would be. I remained amazed for the rest of my life, since this photo hung in every home where Chuck and I lived, and I never saw a need for such a blissful image. Maybe the girl in that photo did float, like a ghost, over our entire relationship. Our marital relationship was more beautiful and mysterious than I ever fully recognized. I thought most married people had something very similar to what we had, but I am aware now that I was wrong.

Our brief honeymoon was underwhelming, except for the sexual aspects and the love we felt. Claytor Lake was the closest body of water where we could enjoy a long weekend. We did hit the beach, but it was cloudy and totally unmotivating. We went to the only movie in town, but it was awful. We even went bowling because we were sure we were supposed to do something out of bed.

We became instant adults in our own eyes. Our afford-able apartment was near our families, and they helped us furnish it and move in. Allie, my teacher friend, had helped us work out the budget because I told her my par-ents had always lived paycheck to paycheck. I wanted to be responsible and make a workable plan.

The landlady was charging sixty-five dollars a month, but I had budgeted only sixty. We compromised on sixty-two fifty. I had my *100 Ways to Cook Hamburger* cookbook and was confident about being a housewife.

I had my job at Parks and Recreation for the summer, and Chuck would sell Fuller brushes. We had an envelope system for bills. Each bill should be within our budgeted amount and when it was not, we had to borrow from the grocery money or, usually, the Christmas fund. We were very honest and careful. When my math-major husband made a mistake of one hundred dollars in the checkbook, I was disillusioned; I tried to appear graceful in my accep-tance of his error. I realized I could hold this over his head for a lifetime, and was ashamed that I even thought about it. The affordable car we purchased from the pastor was a real clunker; but it usually worked if you plugged the battery into the ceiling-light socket on the porch. The porch was our car's garage. Chuck had to catch a ride to school on days the car did not work. Since our apartment was on the highway leading to the college, it was convenient. Sometimes, he had to carpool.

When he began to bring me stories from single guys in the carpool, I broke down in tears. I assumed he was telling them about our sex life since he was hearing about theirs. I argued with him, but finally believed him when he said, "They don't even notice I am not talking because they are enjoying their own stories so much."

Our sex life was so new and precious that I did not want it exposed. I had even imagined that Chuck might prefer to be single again when he learned about other guys' experiences. I was wrong.

Chuck's summer job, and his lack of sales ability, caused him to spend too many days showing his mom wonderful Fuller Brush bargains to buy. Many of the young females on his sales route only let him come into their homes to get the free perfume and lotion samples. They bought nothing. He tried to hide his failure from me.

By the middle of summer, Sandy came through with a job for him. Encyclopedia Britannica was developing computer-training programs for teaching math to children, and Chuck became a writer of them. By the end of summer, I had a brief stint as a writer of the math glossary. I could draw the geometric figures once Chuck told me how many sides/angles each had, and I checked out my written definitions with him as well. A math major was a much better-educated employee than I, but we worked together compatibly.

As fall term began, I was teaching fifth grade instead of sixth. One day, a group of serious-looking adults called me out of my classroom. An opening had come up at the high school; the art teacher was retiring. These supervisors had noticed my dual-degree qualifications in both art and English.

I agreed to take the job if the art teacher would consult with me before I began. I needed to review what the curriculum usually contained. My little fifth graders seemed disappointed when I told them my plan to leave. I knew I would miss their innocence and trust, but I was secretly thrilled to be teaching art to older children.

My new carpool was a much shorter drive to the high school, and there were only two of us. Janice, my driver, had been a high school basketball star I knew. She also happened to be the other senior-class sponsor; we were expected to develop the senior play and senior prom. I really liked that more than bus and playground duty at the elementary school.

Life was really getting better, but some days Chuck relieved his serious studies with games of bridge at the college store. One day, he came home late and admitted this shortcoming. I was the typical working wife by then, as I became upset by my serious work while he played. Our marriage was not perfect, even though I wanted it to look that way. I was attempting to perfect my marriage in Mom's preferred style—work before play. Sometimes I forgot to make room for playtime. This was a family pattern.

I enjoyed teaching art. I even taught some commercial art, like sign painting and lettering, that the students had never had. The younger students received instruction in creativity, originality, and color mixing. I was absolutely shocked when one boy kept bringing various shades of brown to match purple, or other shades I used as color-matching samples. Since he was so serious, I soon realized he was color-blind. He and his family had never been aware of it.

Children's individual needs and problems were frequently neglected in this farming community. I tried to be sensitive to these differences. One principal told me, "Don't you ever harm one of their children, or you will regret it. The parents may often beat them, but you may not touch them."

I changed some things when I could. I asked a senior boy one day what he might do after high school, and he said, "Gonna drive the school bus." I asked him what else he might do and he said, "Gonna drive the school bus." I dropped the subject after that.

One of my college-bound students plagiarized part of his senior theme, and I failed him. I was regretful when I found it was the son of the PTA president. The father was angry when he met with me, but I was able to persuade him I did his son a favor. If his son had to repeat twelfth grade, it would cost him only a little time. The impact on his life would be negligible and certainly far less than the dire consequences being faced by military-college seniors who were being expelled for plagiarism. In the end, Roger, this man's son, was able to pass senior English, but with a significantly lower grade. Nonetheless, he was still admitted to his chosen college.

My seniors were allowed to write their senior themes on future employment goals if they wished. I received some well-written, practical papers and few literary gems. Senior themes had previously been limited to literary analysis. One girl, who wrote about becoming a beautician/hair stylist, later met me in her local training program where I went for a less expensive haircut. She told me she had me "under her control" and threatened to do bad things to my hair for those "darned pop quizzes" she hated. I had used pop quizzes for testing the seriousness of a student's attention to the course. I liked the students who kept pace with me and challenged me.

The high school teaching was sometimes a delight. I enjoyed supervising tryouts for the senior play; Janice selected the play. Senior-prom chaperoning made Chuck and me feel as if we were high school sweethearts, rather than newlyweds. We dressed in our best and looked really attractive among these slightly younger versions of couples.

When I was asked to chaperone a house party for one wealthy senior, I immediately refused. I knew I would be expected to look the other way, and I would not be good at that. I wanted the seniors to like me, but I would not condone bad behavior.

By the end of my school year, Chuck had lined up his new career at the Department of Defense in computer programming. This was a new field, and he and Bill, his favorite bridge partner, would start together in Radford, Virginia. Our planned move to that area allowed us to shop for apartments in Blacksburg or Christiansburg, as well as other surrounding areas. I chose Blacksburg, the home of Virginia Tech, since there were so many cheaper apartments.

I had a couple of last-minute scares before Chuck became employed. He had overstudied for one final math exam. The teacher said he should have flunked him because he "blanked out" during the testing. Roanoke College was only graduating five math seniors. Chuck had been an A student all along the way; therefore, his teacher exercised compassion in allowing him to graduate.

My other scare was when Chuck said he would be eligible for starting as a GS-5, but would wait on being offered a GS-7 with a better salary. I was uncertain, but his self-confidence in pursuing government service at a higher level paid off. He was offered the higher position. We were two happy people.

I found a very inexpensive apartment for us to move into immediately. I did not notice some undesirable aspects of this apartment complex because I was inexperienced in so many ways. The landlord was charming to me when he heard my husband was coming to town for a government job. I was to later learn that most families there were college students at Virginia Tech. Most of the small children had stay-at-home moms since the dads were students in college.

At the apartment complex, I began to be included in the wives' social relationships. Soon, I stopped using birth control; I fully retired after only two years of teaching and readied myself for our family planning by babysitting for others occasionally.

I also found social connections through our new church. Since Chuck had been a Methodist, I decided that we could try another brand of religion. It seemed only fair since he had followed me into my church as a committed member. I learned there was little difference in Southern Methodists and Southern Baptists. Chuck let me know his experience was with Northern Methodists. Apparently, they were more relaxed about everything related to church attendance. I was never a relaxed Baptist.

Since we had both been in a church choir, we decided to join the choir of our new church. We became known very quickly. Chuck had a marvelous singing voice, which I had enjoyed as we sang together in the car. I did not have the ability to carry a tune but had never realized since we always sang in harmony to memorized songs. Now when he wanted to harmonize, I had to stay in the alternative melody. Still, I always wandered over towards the notes he sang and failed. He was usually very forgiving of my shortcomings since he became a recognized soloist.

Chuck may have enjoyed my enthusiasm when we both sang the same tune in the car, so I never noticed much of a problem until Easter. During the Hallelujah Chorus of the "Messiah," I had so many voices from which to choose. I probably sang most parts as I randomly followed my favorite voices in and out of the melody. I was unable to stick to my soprano part. The choir director and other singers noticed my lack of direction and ability, but were also very forgiving. Chuck and I seemed compatible even when we had differences.

***

Moving to a better apartment allowed us to fit into a nicer neighborhood that had a greater number of employed people. There were still young couples, but generally these were in traditional-style relationships popular at that time: the husband was the breadwinner. I wanted to be like them. I wanted to be a real homemaker since my income was not needed. I was supposed to get pregnant.

At one point, we became concerned that we might be an infertile couple, so we sought out a specialist who treated me for infertility. I decided to return to work and found a job teaching seventh grade in Pulaski, Virginia. I rode with my friend, another teacher at the same school. This was the best carpool yet.

It must be clear by this time that I was not licensed or trained to drive a car. My family had always been poor and I could not be allowed to use such an asset as the family car for my own needs. Allowing me to drive was too risky. Truthfully, Dad's alcoholism had impacted several cars we owned, and Mom rarely drove. We used public transportation as the bus stop was nearby.

It wasn't until I finally became pregnant that I learned to drive. Pulaski Board of Education made pregnant women quit teaching as soon as they were showing, so I would have several months to learn before the baby was born. We could share one car so Chuck could carpool to work while I shopped for groceries on my own and belong to women's groups.

Since both our families lived nearby in Roanoke, I could also visit them. Our little Volkswagen could go forty-five miles an hour up Christiansburg Mountain. Chuck could make it go faster, but I had more respect for cars than he did. I empathized with our small car's struggle as it climbed the mountain we lived on.

It was an idyllic time for our family when we became three instead of two. Except Michael, our son, had to wear a foot brace at night to correct a malformation in his bone structure. I was devastated; my mother-in-law had to reassure me that he would develop normally. It was comforting when he did seem to reach each marker of development well enough. We enjoyed a mostly carefree life.

Chapter 3

Discovering Family Life

I talked to Baby Michael often, as I wanted to explain things to him. For instance, when we passed apartment buildings I would say, "These are apartment buildings. These are like lots of little houses stacked on top of each other because there are lots of people. See, there are different people in each one." Later, when Michael grew up as an overly talkative young man, I wondered if I had created a problem without recognizing it.

I also wondered, when he was inclined towards fast driving and car accidents, about his father's influence laying Hot Wheels tracks all over the floor. I also wondered about my mother's influence since one of the first toys she gave him was a model car from the Ford dealership. Michael loved how fast and smoothly his toy cars ran, but his favorite thing was removing the wheels. I always put the wheels back on but it took him a while to learn how to do that. He seemed much less motivated to repair the car than to take it apart.

My mother-in-law was a tremendous help with my parenting a first child. She always greeted him with "Hi, doll!" When he learned to talk, he referred to her as his "hi doll" instead of "Grandma." He felt her tremendous love and approval and returned it.

Michael was an easy child for me. He would entertain himself for hours with large wooden puzzles we worked together, or play with his car tracks, racing different cars in competitive practice against each other. As he grew older, I had gatherings of women in my home. He often had many playmates since I led craft groups while the children shared a large playroom downstairs.

Our family was still very active in church because it was easy to take Michael and Chuck with me. It seemed to feel good to each of us as I review my own impressions. Of course my family, unlike Chuck's, had always been active in church and attended regularly.

I was allowed to teach the youth in our new Methodist church. I had to seek the help of one of the Elders since I had been a Baptist. In Worship Service on Sunday morning, we said the Apostles' Creed in unison. I was disturbed by the words "descended into hell," referring to Jesus, because I had never heard this part in my Baptist church.

The Elder explained it as something along the lines of "Jesus had to go into Hades/hell after his death to quickly allow one more chance for the people already there to be saved." I liked this so much better than the Baptist message about our having to save everyone before their death.

I made this a focus of my teaching, and the young people studied the words of the creed to see if we agreed with it. I was told I had gained the respect of many in the church because some adults had learned to quote the words with little understanding. The children I was teaching brought the meaning home to them.

Now I can see this as the beginning of my need to be truthful about my beliefs when I speak within the church body. I prefer being outspoken. I intend to engage others by questioning; however, I can sound as if I am confident of my own position when really, I am uncertain and want dialogue.

I need to be very careful about seeming confident because I have been misunderstood by people for whom I care. My passion speaks loudly, but I do not think I am always right; there is diversity and respect in our dialogue. I prefer this style of applied beliefs as I speak with others. Christians who do not practice some of the most authentic principles that Jesus taught are not Christians, in my opinion. My favorite Christians are those I think of as Jesus' people. Jesus, as described behaviorally, is a wonderful model of how to live a loving life.

My mom and dad did not object to our becoming Methodists, and family life allowed us to visit often. My dad began to suffer from the lung cancer that ultimately took his life,. Still, I treasure memories of my big, strong, masculine dad reaching down to hold a very small hand as he and Michael took a walk.

Michael's impending birth caused me to quit teaching after my sixth month since I was showing; the school system did not allow pregnant women to teach after their pregnancy was visible. I had enjoyed a wonderful year. My class learned very well since I made them play *Hollywood Squares* and other quiz games with the chapter facts in our history book. I also had the students select a favorite student teacher for some classes; they would do the teaching.

Another teacher and I entertained the whole school with our two classes' performance of *A Christmas Carol*. Once again, I was doing theater within a school setting. These children were also from a rural area, and I found them to be appreciative of me and very easy to engage in the classroom.

Some of the oldest children were showing signs of a different maturity. When one girl put answers like "Richard Burton," the famous actor, on her history exam, I was concerned. When the principal told me this thirteen-year-old girl went out with her mother most nights and didn't have time to study, I was alarmed. He said the mother was a prostitute and the girl was probably becoming one.

Public-school teaching was a slice of life that had some undesirable diversity.

Chuck's career at the Radford Arsenal was promising, and he was happy there. He began to examine other career prospects and learned the best future was probably in Washington, DC. Salaries were higher there because of the cost-of-living, but my math-major husband could calculate that the compensation was inadequate. I was not eager to return to my family's experience during the Second World War; being poor was no fun. So, Chuck insisted that his best career advancement would likely be in Norfolk, Virginia.

We did not move to the Norfolk area until after my dad's death. It was a peaceful passing because he consciously planned for his end of life from lung cancer. He had no regrets since he had made an excellent recovery from alcoholism.

Chuck learned that he could advance more quickly as a computer programmer within the Department of Defense if he relocated to an active location in the military hierarchy. Then he could take on supervisory roles. He much preferred programming, but was ambitious and wanted the pay increase advancement would bring.

His meetings with ranking brass were frequent since officers needed to learn the benefits of having some activities programmed. Chuck felt valuable when the goods supplied to ships became automated by a program he wrote. Sometimes there was a program that delivered paychecks to Navy personnel in a timely and efficient manner. He felt really satisfied when he was part of large, automated changes developed by his division.

Eventually, he headed into supervisory roles as more new people were writing programs, and he was a math major with college training for this responsible role. He made progress and liked his job, but liked programming better than supervising others. He had to make sure his employees did their work efficiently.

I remember calls at night interrupting our sleep, until one night I heard a different conversation. I was impressed. "Why do you keep calling me for this? It is your job. You are supposed to know your job. Aren't you? I don't mind helping you with something new, but you are supposed to know this part." I was proud of my husband. He had enough self-respect to set limits with others.

Only occasionally did I hear complaints. Often the complaint was about a contractor who promised an admiral an unrealistic deadline on a project. Chuck would rather tell the admiral that a particular project could not be completed on time.

Contractors employed by private firms were in competition with government workers on many projects. Private workers could promise the moon and push the deadline back. Chuck would be at his same desk for years, while contractors moved around and worked for different companies. Trying to deliver what a contractor promised might create some seriously flawed work without good supervision. Chuck often thought middle management was hell; he did not like being pulled in different directions.

Chuck's advancing career allowed us to buy our first home. I had most of the ideas about what we needed to do. I do not know where these ideas came from since I had never been included on an adult level in any family transactions. I am uncertain what advice I thought my family might have to share, but Chuck's family did display economic success. And I respected Dad Bennett's competence.

Dad Bennett was surprised that I convinced a realtor to sell us a home without the down payment. I assured the realtor that my husband had a reliable job with a salary increase coming soon. That would allow us to pay off a down payment quickly. Apparently, it is illegal for a realtor to advance the down payment on the home he is selling, but I made a good contractual arrangement for our immediate need. We started out in Norfolk as homeowners when the realtor guaranteed the down payment for us.

In addition to this contractual arrangement, I made another about flooding. While we were looking at the home I wanted, I saw a neighbor sitting on her porch, and engaged her in conversation. I was seeking any warnings or cautions she might deliver about our home. She told me the below-ground-level basements on these homes could flood in heavy rains. I took this caution to the realtor and he said if flooding happened, we would need a French drain. I asked how much that would cost, but he was uncertain. I asked him if he would write in our private contract that he would pay for such an expense if flooding occurred. He wrote up all the agreements we negotiated.

In spite of this, I remember the day Chuck and I were using all our towels to wipe up floodwater, unable to keep pace with the water coming into the family room downstairs. I was very hopeful that the realtor would honor his commitment. Even though the contract was not legally drawn, he willingly paid for the drainage ditch. I loved our first home, that trilevel in Norfolk.

As an ambitious homeowner, I wanted to decorate and improve the appearance of our home with my own artistic touches. I did low costs things, such as antiquing old furniture. This was popular at the time. Mom's old dining room table was made to look as though it matched the china cabinet that Dad built for us. The burnished-gold paint I chose seemed to blend well with our new couch covers and drapes.

As I discussed the cost of décor for our new home, I was dismayed to learn that my husband valued new tennis racquets more than new drapes. I believed his priorities were misaligned, but decided I would just show him. I secured a job working from home with a company that did phone surveys. In those days, people frequently answered their phones because there was no way of knowing who was calling. I made my hourly wage at night when Chuck could help with our children.

I paid for the new drapes and slipcovers with the income I earned from my survey work. A friend I had met at the Newcomers Club assisted me in choosing between several contracts with different telephone-survey companies. I actually liked some of the questions I had to ask. Sometimes there were political surveys, and I was interested in the reasons people gave for their political preferences. Once, I had to ask about a medical product being tested, but did not want to ask about all the symptoms of indigestion. Another time, we gave away fried chicken to large families who agreed to be interviewed as people who preferred our brand.

Some people valued being part of a survey. They wanted to believe their opinions helped the company improve their products. Most of us, as employees, knew the company advertised their product was improved based on the responses to these surveys. Often, a new wrapper would announce the product was "new and improved," using words that represented the public opinions expressed in the surveys we collected.

When I supervised one study from an out-of-state company, I felt important. To help me, I hired our pastor and one of the deacons from the church who needed extra income. The survey took place at the Greyhound bus station and was about bus routes and destinations. My teams reported the special problems they found during the surveys.

The first question categorized respondents as male or female. Apparently, there were some cross-dressing men who hung out at the bus station and loved confusing my employees; I was unsure whether my answers were skewed by inaccurate responses from them. I was not asked to supervise a survey again.

Between decorating, women's clubs, survey work, and church, I was well occupied while awaiting the birth of our second child. In the older neighborhood where we lived, the neighbor next door was the Welcome Wagon lady. She befriended me in many other ways, such as offering gardening tips. She gave the shower before Laura, our daughter, was born. I created a flower arrangement the night of the surprise shower because I had become a member of the garden club. My life was filled with artistic beauty.

Maybe this was a substitute for the oil painting I had previously done. Since I missed teaching art, and Chuck had asked me to be a stay-home mom until the children were school age, I wanted to paint again. I found time to do a few paintings, and I remember a couple of them were special to me.

I created an Adam and Eve picture that had the tempta- tion with the apple. One night, a couple of friends came over and teased me about naked people running around in the bushes. We laughed together.

The other was a picture of New Orleans during Mardi Gras. Chuck took it to his office, and a coworker asked to purchase it. When I agreed, Chuck gave it to him as a going-away gift. I was flattered by this attention.

When Laura was finally born in 1968, we decided she would complete our family. One older male and one younger female, four years apart, seemed ideal. Life was almost perfect.

Laura was a very different baby. She was easy and enter- tained herself, but I could not seem to relate well to her. As an example, one day my brother came by and sat on the floor to play with her. He called her a very boring baby because she simply rolled wherever she wanted to go. He could not capture her attention.

The sense that she was only visiting us from a world beyond ours was obvious to me early on, but I did not immediately recognize the feeling. My most vivid memory is the day I sat with her in the grass near our home. This was unusual behavior for me. I watched as she responded to the world around her. The ruffle on her bonnet fluttered slightly, and the grass had small bends in its blades. I watched her carefully. I had not noticed the slight breeze until I saw her eyes respond to the motion. She looked as if she were encountering a windstorm. Were her sensitivities so much greater than mine? I had wondered about her personal experiences before, and I was still confused. She seemed to be in her own world.

Chapter 4

Discovering My Personal Identity

Recognizing how you see yourself and how others see you requires a lifetime of work. I was naturally curious about this and sought to be honest. Someone wanting to take my inventory was welcomed as long as I could learn from it. I could decide if I agreed with the results and wanted to change anything. My mom was my frequent critic, even though she was careful to phrase it as, "You would be a little better if…". It has taken me years to realize I wanted to be like Mom in some ways, but not like her in others. We never had an honest conversation about this because I only criticized my mom internally. Is that honoring my mother according to the Commandments? If not, I failed.

When my dad, at the young age of fifty-six, left Mom a widow, she was eager to be in a relationship with a man. I was embarrassed when she discussed her sexual interests with me. A neighbor once offered to help her with a household project, and then attempted to force himself on her sexually. She had some difficulty handling him, but she ultimately did.

Next, she confided that an attractive choir member expressed interest in a sexual relationship, but was honest enough to say it would not be a committed relationship. I advised her not to be vulnerable since I believed he was so attractive that she would fall for him.

When she began to date two different men, I was pleased that one of them took her dancing and wanted to marry her. He worked for a bank. The second man was a retired Navy man working as a salesman for televisions. She liked him best, but I was unimpressed. Chuck and I had the special role of being witnesses to their marriage when they eloped to North Carolina. (No waiting for weddings there!)

My intuition was correct. It became clear my mother had married a second alcoholic. Dad's life insurance provided them with money for a new home. I gained a stepsister and two stepbrothers. My stepsister lived with them, and the oldest stepbrother was married. The youngest boy was a problem child, but Mom was determined to like him. She seemed more loving in this new family, and she adored her new husband since he was writing a book. He was from the mountains of Tennessee and emphasized his strong family roots. She was also impressed he was retired military and socially active.

I was pleased that Mom was happy. I did not need a mom any longer; therefore, it was not a loss for me when they moved to Tennessee. Living in a new place gave Mom a new identity and freed me to be more myself.

I was still doing marketing surveys for extra income, decorating my house, being a mom to my own two children, and entertaining other families with young children. The arts-and-crafts activities for the sorority were held in my home because of the downstairs room the children enjoyed. The sorority was part of Beta Sigma Phi, a women's business sorority I had joined after I went to Welcome Wagon in Norfolk. I had never been in a sorority and I was really enjoying this focus on community giving, fundraising, and shaping values. I was very active and led the crafts group with a couple of other talented women.

I designed several wooden hanging systems for children's toys. These were sellouts at the craft fair at the mall. I used children's coloring-book pictures as my patterns, and one woman cut the wood into shapes. We had teamwork. When I decided we ought to sell Playboy Calendar pictures of seminude women on our decoupaged wooden plaques, the husbands were thrilled. I found them in Chuck's *Playboy* magazines. These sold better before we had to hide them under our stand at the mall. Censorship was important for public events.

I had never had strong relationships with women before, and this opportunity socialized me. Most of the women became close friends. Our entire family was always involved in church activities. I felt we were an ideal family in our picture-book reality.

The children seemed to have good teachers however, we decided to change churches as we discovered some beliefs and practices did not represent what we believed. Chuck prompted us to leave the Methodist church in Norfolk. We were to pursue a church that fit our family values.

I was angry when our Sunday-morning class collected money for a Christmas basket and the entire class wanted to deliver it. I remembered an experience my dad and I had while delivering a Christmas basket. There was an issue with the family feeling embarrassed of being seen as needy. So I spoke up to our class and told them I thought fewer people delivering the gifts was more respectful, as it was less intrusive. This class seemed to want lots of credit for their giving and every person wanted to be part of visiting the chosen family.

That issue did not create the final break for us, but Chuck's choir experience did. There was a new organist at the church; he was a Black man who also worked at a restaurant on Saturday nights. There had been a complaint that he had fallen asleep during church services. Chuck confronted his choir group with the idea that the man might be having a tough time with two jobs and a tight time schedule. He suggested to the group that the organist being Black was more objectionable to the adults since we had no Black church members. Chuck came home upset about the arguments and discussion that led to dismissing our only Black congregant.

When we were square dancing, we had enjoyed visiting a United Congregational Church, so we decided to try them out for worship. It was timely since they were standing for integration at their church and in the community. Chuck became close to the minister, and we became part of the attempts to racially integrate two churches and some square dance clubs. There were no Blacks in any square dancing. We attracted only one couple to our free demonstrations at the mall, but they did not choose to join. We had better success with the churches.

Chuck had gone to integrated schools in the North, whereas I had only been in segregated schools in the South. I had joined a business sorority named Beta Sigma Phi, and it was also segregated. I had never considered this since it was so familiar. When our chapter had a request for membership from a woman from a foreign country, we learned she was Black and decided to accept her. The citywide controversy over that decision caused great conflict, and we were given a table at the far edge of the room when the next dance occurred. We met our two new Black couples at the door of the dance hall and proudly walked them in to sit with us.

We were experiencing a community in transition, and as we lived our values, we were embraced by the churches we respected. Some of the people we were meeting challenged our beliefs and allowed us to clarify our own values. We began to meet people with a broader sense of religious beliefs.

Several years ago, Laura told me about Lee, a woman who visited our home frequently when Laura was young. Lee and her husband had very different beliefs from Chuck and I. They often talked about their past lives in detail to explain difficulties their family was having. We did not take much of this couple's beliefs seriously, but we did not deny them. We usually respected other people and their beliefs.

Laura says she spoke to Lee at about age four and said, "I see ghosts."

Lee said, "It's okay. Lots of people do."

I did not know about this conversation for many years. Now, Laura shares with me some of her special knowledge. I realize now I did not want to know her spiritual experiences early in her life because it frightened me, and she was too young to explain. I unconsciously blocked it out. Throughout her life, Laura has had some psychic experiences.

Our adjustment to this newest child seemed to create a family with active lives in all directions. I was overwhelmed with a feeling of joy and wondered if we needed to add a foster child to our family. I felt we were so fortunate to have such a loving, small family that we could extend this to others. I knew I had about four more years before my career would resume. Laura and Mike would both be in school by then. There seemed to be plenty of time to add another temporary child or two, as foster parenting was a need brought to the attention of willing church families. Chuck and I talked it over and agreed we were fortunate and able to do this. I called Social Services and set up an interview.

I could not have been more surprised when this social worker told me of the horror stories we might experience if we added a foster child to our family. She seemed unwilling to have us take in another child. She emphasized a recent placement in which the child was a fire starter, and the family suffered chaos and danger. I resisted a bit, knowing there were many good placements within foster families. However, I was persuaded by the possibility of negative consequences, since I was feeling so much love for my two children.

Reflecting on this sequence of events, I realize this was ultimately a fortuitous turn of events. Around that time, Michael's teacher called to report that he possibly had learning problems that needed attention. I tried to explain away his holding a book upside down since he had just started public school. She pointed out that all the other children were doing it the correct way, even though they too, had just started school.

Chuck accompanied me to the optometrist who specialized in treating these problems. Both of us were amazed when we saw Michael reading the eye chart; he skipped several lines without noticing. He was to read line by line, but his eyes went from "the car" in one line of text to "the car" several lines later, without his noticing the skipped lines in between.

We were told what the treatment would cost and I was dismayed we might have to find money in our current budget to pay for it. I questioned the doctor about what techniques they used. He kindly explained what was needed, and I realized I could do the exercises with Michael by myself. Mike had visual dyslexia, and it was even more obvious when he was asked to draw a square with intersecting lines corner to corner. He drew each line separately in order to meet in the middle instead of crossing straight from one corner to the opposite one. His center point was really off-center, and I realized how he saw shapes in different configurations than I did.

Many years later, I realized my brother and I had a similar problem, which had remained undiagnosed. Neither of us received help, but I overcame or outgrew mine; his was more severe. He had extreme reading difficulty early in life whereas I could never pass a speed-typing test in high school. My eyes would also skip to same-word patterns close by in the text, as Michael's responses had demonstrated.

Michael and I worked together easily since we both understood the difficulty he was having. Solutions that had been explained to us were successful, and we were both motivated.

Learning disabilities were also diagnosed in Laura after she began public school. Laura had auditory dyslexia, and we were told that this was a rare condition that had few known strategies for remediation. Both my children, with learning problems, qualified for some programs within the Parks and Recreation Department. These were designed to assist them with hand-eye coordination, creativity, and socialization.

Our two children seemed to develop greater self-esteem as a result of their willing participation. However, the enrollment of other children similar to them was minimal. Most children were grouped together by likeness; so, rather than my children getting the help they needed, they were a help to others with greater challenges.

Chuck and I were pleased the children had learned compassion, but we did not realize how giving to others was a family style we modelled. Laura wanted to learn sign language to help the deaf children, and Michael wanted to tutor others as they both developed greater self-confidence. Underlying this, however, was a lack of confidence when they associated with those who were recognized as bright and talented. Neither Chuck nor I had ever been recognized as above average, though maybe we might have been. Educational systems and successful people often ignore others who are adapting rather than competing; our children seemed normal.

Once again, we thought of adding to our family when presented an opportunity when Mike was eleven years old and Laura was seven. A family from our church had fostered older children, and the social worker contacted me to ask about them. I was able to explain to her that this couple was ending their marriage and under stressful conditions that would probably preclude them taking a new foster child. I was curious and asked about the boy who needed a placement.

I was told that Danny was entering his last year of high school and would not be eligible for foster care as he would turn eighteen in March. Foster care ended on your eighteenth birthday unless you were under family supervision. Fostering him sounded like a short-term project, which made it very desirable. Also, Danny was a painter who had some business ventures of his own that gave him income. He had his own car and was very self-sufficient.

Chuck and I talked about it and decided to foster Danny. We discussed this with the children, and everyone seemed agreeable. The weekend Danny moved into his own bedroom, we had a church picnic and he seemed shy and quiet. We attempted to make him comfortable, and others seemed to like him. One of his first questions to me was whether he should roll his pairs of socks together for the laundry. I didn't understand, but he explained that most foster homes had a preference since socks that were separate often were lost in the wash. I liked his plan and we, as a family, adapted this style with great success since our family had a need not to have to replace socks.

When the social worker told me Danny's only problem was a girlfriend, I said, "Oh, that's okay; we can handle that."

Danny eloped with the girlfriend soon after his senior year began. I had helped him finance new tires for his car. No thoughts about his crossing state lines into North Carolina with this girlfriend to get married had ever occurred to me.

We did not meet Danny's girlfriend until after her mother had the marriage annulled. Apparently, she was underage for marriage in Virginia, and the legalities of marrying in North Carolina were also a problem. The marriage was annulled, and the girl returned home to her family. Danny returned to us, having missed too many days of school to graduate.

It was fortunate that some teachers did not keep accurate absentee records; we reenrolled him and began helping him finish his last year of high school. He only had three classes. Chuck went to woodshop classes with Danny many nights since the high school was nearby. My husband learned something about cabinetmaking when they collaborated on a record cabinet for our collection. I helped with English. His teacher was not naïve; she knew I had taught English, and Danny had too few note cards for his senior theme. "We" passed English with only a D, which Danny enjoyed frequently teasing me about. One of Danny's friends helped him with government class. With all this assistance, Danny graduated, and his parents stayed at our house for the occasion.

The social worker who placed Danny with us said foster parents had to respect the biological parents' connection to their own child. Faye and Scott Kepley seemed to be reasonable parents that weekend…until Sunday, when they began drinking. Everyone understood that they would leave and return to their own home before drinking too much. This was a satisfactory first meeting for all of us parents.

Next in our family drama, Trish, Danny's girlfriend, was pregnant. Danny planned to enter the Army in order to have health-insurance coverage for the prenatal planning and birth. He was still under contract for the Army when Trish decided to terminate the pregnancy. Her mother did not want to face this choice, and I was selected to drive her to the clinic for her procedure. Danny accepted Trish's decision without complaint. The cradle Danny built in woodshop was given to Chuck's brother since they were expecting their first child. I was living the couple's crisis and did not register approval or disapproval. These were not my choices.

Even though we had known Danny such a short time, when he left for the service, he seemed like a family member. We went to his military graduation from basic training and barely recognized him. He had been stressed and physically ill.

Danny was, fortunately, assigned to a base near us, and returned to our home. He began to drive about forty-five miles to Fort Eustis each day. He worked in the motor pool and was quite talented at keeping the equipment and trucks running. He often complained that the other guys sat under a tree while he did all the work.

I reminded him, "If you are always the best one, they may continue to behave this way."

Danny did not express confidence in himself or his abilities, but we appreciated his many talents and his self-sufficiency. He only left our home to move into an apartment near the base with an Army friend, after he and I had words. I can't remember what the issue was at that time, but I do remember him being so upset.

He was extremely unhappy when his sergeant called him out in front of morning lineup, "Your momma called, and you need to call her. She is worried about you."

I was having adjustment pains. My children were much younger, and I had never raised a teen or launched an adult. My experience came quickly. Our family life had seemed ideal enough to add another child, particularly an older, more independent one. In hindsight, I wonder how chaotic things actually were, since drama with Danny obscured our vision. We did not even notice Michael beginning to doubt his sexual identity. Both Laura and he were adjusting to Danny's friends coming in and out of our home.

Chuck enjoyed Danny's male maturity, such as it was. Laura received attention and protection from all Danny's older male friends as she grew into her own maturity. Her own brother often irritated her. Michael's issues caused me to seek therapy for him, and the counselor affirmed Mike's ambivalence about heterosexual relationships. His counselor protected Michael's confidentiality and would not tell me more.

My initial interest in Danny's assigned social worker had blossomed into full-blown admiration when I heard about the opportunity to become a licensed clinical social worker. She was able to tell me some of the practical side of this kind of work. At church, the minister's wife had signed up to go to graduate school in social work. She had learned that a program at Norfolk State University could lead to licensure and independent practice. This seemed too good to be true! I would almost be a psychiatrist!

By this time, we had become members of the United Church of Christ and moved to Virginia Beach. Our new minister inspired us since he was interested in group dynamics and was leading the church in consciousness raising. We were in a couples' group, and I was asked to lead the women.

This minister was our model for questioning the church's values and practices. I felt free to be myself. When the church board asked for me to become a deaconess, I was honored. As I explored the vows I would take, I found wording with which I did not agree. I asked if I could skip or deny that part. When the head of the board confronted me about my issues with the contract, I stood my ground. I would not compromise my newly formed ideas. The man who was head of the board announced my rejection, and I was saddened to think I did not qualify.

I was active in a jail-ministry program called Outmate Outreach. Chuck and I tutored at the jail for inmates to gain their graduate equivalency diploma (GED). I had a team of college students under my supervision. All of this was quite invigorating since church was a place of service for us. We felt kinship and alliances with our close associates and friends who shared our own chosen values.

I asked the minister's wife if I could copycat her in the program at Norfolk State, and she wished me well. I soon called the college about the program; I was very timid about my request since I had poor undergraduate grades. It is another remarkable coincidence that the dean was away at the time; the dean's wife answered the phone. She told me I could apply and be accepted on a temporary basis. If I could not keep a B average, I would be dismissed from the program.

I immediately applied to Old Dominion University in Norfolk to take prep courses that I selected. Statistics and abnormal psychology were known to be difficult courses, and I took both the next semester to improve my study habits and grade average. Chuck agreed to take on more responsibility with the children at home when I studied.

I have often wondered if I would have been a more attentive and better mom to my children if we had not fostered Danny, and if I had not been so eager to go to graduate school.

Danny had a new dimension to his life. He was dating Tina, and both Chuck and I liked her. She was a better influence on our children since Danny was more stable with her. Tina's parents had kept foster children for many years, and perhaps she had more familiarity with a foster child's experiences. She could understand both sides of our relationship with Danny. Danny's sister, Libby, lived as a foster child with Tina's parents. He took me to meet her.

As we began to explore his family history, I learned that, in his family, there were three other children who had been in and out of foster care and in different homes. Barbara Jean had also lived with Tina's parents at one time. The two youngest children, Tracy and Jeff, never stayed in foster care long. They were eager to return to their parents, while the three older children had been taken into care earlier and more frequently. Danny told us vivid stories of his parents' neglect and abuse. I never laughed with him, as he would often laugh, particularly at his father's outrageous drunken episodes.

Tina had been living outside of her parents' home with girlfriends, and the situation became difficult. She moved in with us for a while, until she and Danny married. No doubt, Danny was on the rebound from the relationship with Trish, but we were so pleased that Tina seemed to love him, and he was happier.

On their wedding day, Chuck and I determined that Trish was trying to reach Danny by phone. We could not allow this last-minute chaos, so we kept him busy until evening. I was feeling very guilty as his friend walked me down the aisle. My intuition told me that Danny did not love Tina enough. Maybe the marriage was ill-fated, but I desired this relationship for Danny. Tina was an independent and loyal young woman. She would make a great marriage partner for Danny.

Today, I have much less guilt because I consider this a happy part of our family life. Danny and Tina had two precious daughters who were a blessing for both Chuck and me. This larger family was a rich experience for each of us. Tina was also a great partner for Danny's business, and Chuck invested several thousand dollars in Dominion Décor, the name they chose for his paint-contracting business.

During this period in my life, I was gratified to find my life's purpose. Graduate school led me to recognize my personal prophecy as a young girl was predictive. I wanted to be a psychiatrist, but I actually meant a family therapist in the practical sense of my ability to serve others. I completed a dual-track credential for systems and families. In social work, this allows one to practice counseling, or lead agencies and community programs. I wanted to be ready for whatever life offered me.

Upon graduation, I interviewed for several positions. The court position was to serve under a judge. When I tested well, the clerk said, "The judge will love you because you are a Baptist, and you went to Baylor." I walked out of the office knowing I did not want the job since it was serving under another Baptist.

When I interviewed at a family agency, I ignored that Catholic Family Services might constitute similar problems of religious conflict for me, and I accepted that position. I was quite pleased at how I answered one tough question: How will you feel being non-Catholic in our agency? I said, "Men doctors don't have the babies, but many think they are well-informed about how to do it." I was surprised they wanted me, but I did know that my potential supervisor was the only other non-Catholic at the agency, and she was well respected. That was a comfort.

Jeanette Franklin was a wonderful supervisor. I admired her, and she was my role model. In one of our first supervisory sessions, I told the first outright lie I ever remember telling. She asked me if I had sent out the letters I had written, introducing myself to agency clients. I could not disappoint my boss, so I immediately said yes. That lie made me feel so very bad internally that I vowed not to ever do it again.

Having graduated and been hired, I liked myself and felt such renewed self-esteem that it was easy to tell the truth after that. (I am very good at distracting, avoiding, or changing the subject, so the statement "The whole truth, so help you God" has to be avoided.) I justified my lie by saying to myself it would only stay a lie briefly, since I sent the letters out promptly, and the lie was now truth. My supervisor never found out, but I knew.

Working full-time, for both Chuck and me, caused some family adjustments. I was not available for transporting the children to their activities, but we were fortunate that a neighbor could get Laura to dance lessons, and Michael could ride his bike to most things. I cooked mostly on weekends and made meals for the week. Chuck checked on the children's activities and did more co-parenting.

Michael's visual-learning disability had been treated, and he was making remarkable progress while also being active in drama class and Boy Scouts.

Laura's challenges with auditory learning were not understood and she began to feel less secure about her own abilities. A seventh-grade teacher put up a class evaluation, and Laura was at the bottom. I spoke to the teacher about Laura's difficulty, and she corrected her public list by putting Laura near the top. After that, we asked that she be placed in a more appropriate class experience, and she was moved. I did not understand what the public school was doing with her. None of us did.

Dance classes helped Laura's self-esteem, and she was quite talented. She had several solo performances when her dance class had its recital during her senior year of high school. Her physical development advanced beyond her maturity, and she attracted lots of sexual attention from boys in the years between junior and senior high.

Neither of my children, unfortunately, shared their traumatic experiences with me. A family-therapy appointment when Laura was about fifteen years old brought some issues to the surface. Mother's new husband had sexually traumatized Laura when the children visited my mother for a week. Mom and her husband were living in Tennessee then, and we had not gotten well acquainted with their lives.

Since Mom had married a second alcoholic, she had begun to drink with him. When this story was presented in family therapy, we were to wait until the next week to see what Laura wanted to do. I did not wait. I called Child Protective Services, and they sent a worker to interview Laura privately at school. Laura decided not to initiate a court process because that would hurt her grandmother too much.

I confronted my mother about the charges, but she denied them and covered for her husband as best she could. Though I barely knew my stepsister, I knew her children sometimes visited with Mother and Bob. I questioned my stepsister about the safety of her children; she cautiously told me she never left them with her father.

I had never been very close to my mom, but that situation drove a wedge between us that was keenly felt. Mother made many attempts to bring me back into acceptance of her life with Bob, but nothing worked. Much later, I received a card from Bob, generally apologizing for how he "may have hurt me in any way."

I called and spoke with him to say that his apology needed to be to Laura. It was interesting when he said he could not do that because the lawyer warned him he would be responsible for whatever came up after his admission. Bob had avoided the watch list for pedophiles, which made me wonder about the fairness of our laws and court system.

It was easy for the entire family to avoid further contact with my stepfather, but this remained difficult for my mother. Having once acknowledged his responsibility, sometimes she denied it. It seemed easier for her to deny as she grew older.

Laura shares much more of her personal history with me today, and we have discussed when she had sexual relationships by choice. Her advanced development caused her much conflict, and she seemed to have sexual experiences earlier than desirable. When we went to the doctor and discovered she had herpes, she was devastated and had trouble identifying the person responsible. She had wanted to begin a lifeguard job at the rec center, but could not complete the training because of her diagnosis. Her self-esteem remained fragile, and we tried to offer support in various ways.

Laura began working at sixteen, through her own efforts, and that gave her greater confidence. She really liked having her own income, and when she went on the senior trip to New York with her school group, she made fantastic buys in the Garment Center. My daughter was growing up.

Michael and Laura, both, continued to attend church with us, and our family had core strength through our beliefs. When Mike was sixteen, I was the youth leader of the teens, and he wanted to disclose to them that he was gay. I asked him not to risk that, since I felt he needed acceptance and validation after waiting so long. He had seen a counselor, my coworker Tom, who honored Michael's confidentiality when we met for his evaluation. We discussed that Michael would continue to clarify whether he was actually gay or not.

Maybe it was totally wrong for me to interfere, and I do question my behavior. When Michael began college, he developed the best relationships he had ever had. He formed a romantic relationship with a boy from North Carolina, and they attracted attention by living together in the dorm. When Michael learned he had HIV, he was devastated. He believed all his new friends would give up on him for fear of catching AIDS. This was another traumatic event for him.

Chuck and I learned that the college told Michael he could not live in the dorm with a male roommate. Mike and Chuck talked, and Chuck agreed to let Mike move off campus. I admired Chuck's support of our son, but I thought Mike should stay on campus and live alone. Mike's teacher in social work told him he could not be a counselor as a gay man. He and I discussed the difficulties he might face, and I offered him support by not agreeing with his teacher.

Amazingly, Michael remained in school despite the difficulties. He switched to a business major, which upset me. I thought he might be a good counselor. Michael and his romantic partner separated, and it appeared as though he began a series of sexual relationships. We were living in Virginia Beach, and his college was near Roanoke; we did not know what he was actually experiencing.

Michael's drug-abuse began right around that time. He believed he would not live long with his HIV status, and he gave up caring. His romantic partner had been dating girls before he met Mike, and they discussed how he might be better off had he returned to that choice while he still could. Mike lost some friends, a lover, and his health. I am surprised he stayed in school and continued college. Ferrum

College had a reputation for helping students with learning disabilities; therefore, Michael had a chance of success.

He also became a math tutor and had a job assisting a girl who was in a wheelchair. He was very compassionate in his care of her. College was the best educational experience he had ever had. He almost graduated from Ferrum.

There were at least two important factors that impacted Michael's leaving college before graduating. He wanted to follow my path into social work and counseling, but at Ferrum he was told he would not be able to do that work. Then, he had to do a job placement for graduation, and the place where he worked suspected him of theft within the store. I never wanted to connect this with his new drug-abuse habit; I never was certain what occurred.

Michael came home and planned to complete his degree locally. All the confusion about education and work was difficult to assess since he was an active drug user with poor relationships and out-of-control behavior. As loving parents, we may have found it easy to deny reality.

After Chuck died, I was the only parent. I had to take stronger action. When Michael forged checks on my account, I took the legal steps that led to his incarceration. There were other times in which I stood up for him, and he was enrolled in programs that helped. We attended an excellent family program in Virginia Beach and, once, we even worked at Salvation Army as group leaders.

Chapter 5

Discovering Diversity

My career was very satisfying at Catholic Family Services since I had been inspired by the Baptist church during my younger years to have a mission. In my youth, I felt I might be a missionary because we Baptists were responsible for saving the world. Over time, I came to believe differently, but I always knew I needed to serve God in a significant way. In my role as a family therapist, I could perhaps affect great positive outcomes in family interactions. Being a foster parent created a larger family for Chuck and me, and this seemed to make us feel as if we could have a special influence on many others.

When Chuck and I first married, I asked him to promise that we would always help others through giving to the Christian Children's Fund. We were so poor in the beginning, but we did it. I had written our selected children, each from some foreign country, for eighteen years. I had respect for the foreign translators and liked hearing about each child's culture or religious ideals. Chuck objected strongly when I told him it was his time to take over this duty.

When I quit corresponding with his mother by letter years before, he had also objected, but he had to measure up to my standards or explain himself. Tangling with me might be difficult, but he could not possibly undertake a struggle with me *and* his mom or dad. They were not churchgoers, but did believe in the humanitarian ventures we undertook.

His family was not truly happy about our taking in Danny, but they never questioned us. No one in their family had ever reached far beyond the immediate family circle; their devotion for each other looked better than what I had learned in church. They were a loving family, but they did not lend support to anyone other than family. I led Chuck to follow my model, and he did.

My dad, the policeman, had done secret work in humanitarian ways. Mom helped only the "good guys" and had little patience or compassion for some of the "undeserving" poor. She was clear about who those undeserving were.

Mom's best friend was a Mormon, and she studied their sacred texts and went to some of their services. Once, she became angry at her group of Baptist church ladies for criticizing the Mormons. She had invited some Mormon singers to church, but they were not welcomed by the congregation. The ladies were uncertain of the Mormons' claim to be Christians, since many of the ladies believed the Mormon church taught some dubious beliefs.

In 1979, when I started at Catholic Family Services, we had five immediate family members, and Tina, Danny's second wife, made it six. Danny was twenty-two, Michael was fifteen, and Laura was eleven. All of us lived together and shared family values. Life seemed stable at home, and I could devote myself to a chosen career. This career served my desire to share my values whenever the client seemed to share my beliefs.

The agency did not have a medical consultant, but I felt we needed a psychiatrist. My supervisor, Jeanette, chose Dr. David Rosen, and I was to learn even more about treatment aspects under his guidance.

The power structure of the agency was from the top, down, and we counselors were at the satellite office. We provided income for the family-services part of the agency programs, which were free to other Catholics. We saw ourselves as unappreciated stepchildren being criticized for making too little money for the real Catholic families. Having Dr. Rosen on staff legitimized our counseling work to some degree, and I liked that. We focused on mental health issues rather than religious values.

One of my clients was married to the owner of a Ford dealership, and she was interested in an EAP (employee-assistance program) for the business. I was offered that training and I became the director of that program while I continued to see clients at Catholic Family Services. My career was blossoming in many directions, and I could see a bright future after I finished satisfying my three or four years of needed supervision to become licensed.

This agency did set some standards that were difficult for me to obey. Our case notes were seldom seen by supervisors, and I occasionally chose to counsel clients according to their own standards, rather than the agency's religious doctrine. Under these divergent circumstances, I was a true social worker with the client's best interest guiding me.

One very special client became pregnant by a neighbor and decided to have an abortion. I did not reveal this in my notes. Agency guidelines were very clearly against abortion, and I attempted to dissuade her, not by agency policy, but by her own beliefs. She had two teenage sons; then, because she was pregnant with their first child, she married a military man training for the astronaut program. That marriage ended unhappily. She refused to consult with her neighbor about her current pregnancy, and he never knew he had fathered a child. I was sad for her because she felt the same shame she had felt in her unhappy marriage. This was another unwed pregnancy, and she had to face the consequences alone.

Since she was divorced, it felt as though she was the only one doing anything wrong. She had been a nurse in Vietnam during the war, and she had sex only one time with her child's father, right before he flew off to a war zone, from which he did not think he would return alive. She had lovingly comforted him, and the sexual encounter produced a pregnancy. She blamed only herself for the sexual alliance.

She raised two boys alone, with different fathers. Eventually, during ongoing counseling, I had to add to her personal pain by advising her to let the oldest son visit his dad. The older son wanted to know his father, and he needed to do that. Much later, I felt some resolution; her oldest son returned home by personal choice. His father had taken little interest in him, and the child grew to fully appreciate his mother.

One other woman I saw at the agency had planned to have an abortion, and I did not attempt to change her mind. She had no desire to ever be a mother, and she was unable to show much emotion or caring of any kind in many human situations. I had only seen her briefly, but she seemed to have some significant relationship problems. She may have been schizophrenic and in need of medication. She did not care for herself well enough to be able to raise a child.

Since I had always valued having a wanted and loved child above continuing an unwanted pregnancy, it was easy for me to allow her to make her own decision without questioning it. I was so pleased when Roe V. Wade made abortion legal. Personally, I believed that this was a Christian perspective. Jesus and God seem to teach about love's importance, not the survival of physical bodies. Abortion was about physical embodiment for me, rather than spiritual reality. I did not believe a fetus was a human life until birth.

I attempted to compassionately serve these women and did not make notes in their charts. Any evidence of my allowing abortions or my own approval of these actions were damning at this Catholic agency. Premarital classes taught only the rhythm method for birth control, which largely depended on abstinence. Most of the couples decided on noncompliance without much guilt.

Every day, I was hearing about infidelities, bad marriages, and unhappy families. Fears and uncertainty haunted my sexual ardor as I unconsciously learned that men wanted too much sex, and we women had to develop self-control. Self-control became a lack of arousal. "Sexy" was no longer a good word for a married woman like me. Unconsciously, I was unwillingly returning to the shame I had learned in the Baptist church. Sexual passion was not addressed in my premarital counseling.

All of this was a sharp contrast to my confident and aroused honeymoon personality. I had given Chuck a *Playboy* magazine subscription for our first anniversary, and he really took the articles seriously. He kept encouraging me into greater sexual expression, but I resisted. When he brought a vibrator home from a business trip to Washington, DC, I was furious.

"Who do you think I am? I never saw one of those things in my entire life."

Chuck was the only person to explain to me that boys and men masturbate frequently. He encouraged me to learn to satisfy myself in some way.

I listened and thought about it. I loved my husband, and I could see that he made a rational complaint about my reduced interest in sexually responding. We had no crises in our marriage, and I wanted to avoid future difficulties; therefore, I followed his lead in this matter. Our marital relationship improved as we enjoyed easier closeness and spontaneity.

Chuck had undergone a vasectomy because his older brother had told him about choosing this easier birth-control method. I no longer had to carry the burden of birth control since he took on more responsibility. That seemed a loving act.

Fidelity was something I had taken for granted in our marriage, but Chuck's infrequent business trips caused me some concern. We had been in highly sexualized environments in our early marriage and had discussed temptations. We both felt immune from that danger. Square-dancing conventions had wild after-parties, and the sorority brought together happy and unhappy married folks at all their social gatherings. We saw people go astray.

After one sorority luau, a bunch of people left to go skinny-dipping. We did not go. And then there was the party at which Chuck and I had difficulty. We were hosting for New Year's and, as always, there was competition over a football game on TV. I was determined Chuck would lead the men to turn it off and join us for the early-evening drinking, dancing, and socializing. There had been lots of plans made, but Chuck chose the alternative—watching football with the men.

After the final play of the game, I was furious. Chuck had been drinking a lot. In the stories I heard later, Chuck was kissing one of the sorority sisters while they were dancing. These events and stories occupied much of my headspace for an extended period.

I had my first doubts about our marriage. I made it clear to Chuck that he could have her or anyone else he desired, but he could not have me. He needed to be clear because there was only an either-or choice. Both was not an option. I am surprised how I had the confidence to cover this same ground several times, making him angry each and every time, but it was that important to me.

At the next party, I was a little more flirty, and I think a man got the feeling that I was signaling. He was dancing with me, and he said, "You better not turn that bottom towards me one more time, or I will do something with it." I heeded that warning.

Counseling at the office also made me more aware of the dangers of infidelity in marriage. Several strong Catholic mothers I saw for counseling were putting up with various infidelities in their marriages in order to raise their families as they wished. One woman told me a strange tale of sexually manipulating her husband. He was very careful about her spending, and when he complained too much about the grocery bill, she said, "I only need to start unbuttoning my blouse. He quits complaining immediately."

One case was very difficult for me since I was shocked and had to control my reaction. The couple came in for counseling, and she complained that she did not like their habit of swapping partners during gatherings with other couples. She had been putting up with it, but wanted it to stop. In order to gather my thoughts and cover my reactions, I asked her to tell me more. She told me about the partners her husband chose; consequently, she was left with that person's mate.

I asked her which man she might choose if she were the one to initiate the choice. As she began to think about this, I could see more discomfort in her husband's expression, so I encouraged her to continue. I consciously wanted both of them to know that choosing others as sexual partners might have unpleasant side effects. I was not surprised that this couple never returned for more counseling, but I was curious about what changes, if any, they may have made.

Sometimes we can be immune to others' human behavior, and sometimes it is so obvious. Chuck and I were invited to a home at the beachfront when a new woman in our church group hosted a Halloween party. The house was gorgeous, and the entire gathering seemed a bit above our usual social environment. The guests and their costumes were marvelous. We had chosen *Star Trek* costumes; we were green and ugly. I immediately regretted this, but Chuck seemed to be having a good time. The beautiful people were wearing harem outfits with lots of pretty, bare skin. The other men were in white silk, and some wore turbans.

As the evening continued, people were leaving the main room and coming back much happier. It occurred to me that there might be illegal refreshments upstairs, and we weren't being invited. I asked Chuck if we should leave soon, and we did. He was always cautious about his security clearance at work and avoided compromising situations.

Over our many years of marriage, we each knew the other was faithful. Chuck's proof to me, among other things, was his saving his daily allowance for expenses when he had a three-week trip to Hawaii. He used this money to fly me over to spend a week with him. He had arranged to rent a friend's condo, and this was one of the most wonderful trips I ever had. Everyone at the Hawaii offices knew about his devotion to me since one of the women at the office made a real lei for me. He met me at the plane and placed this beautiful, flowering work of art around my neck in traditional style.

In order for me to show more love to Chuck, I had to break some bad habits. One bad habit was pushing him away when he attempted to kiss me while I was doing something important, like the dishes. How stupid was that! I loved to be kissed on the back of my neck, but just as he was attempting to do that, I pulled away. As a girl, I honored the saying "Work first, play later," until one day it occurred to me that the work was never done. I had to correct my stance and put a priority on love first, duty second. It was a major change for me within my marriage. My intuition was confused about what was truly desirable.

Over our years together, Chuck had to lead me into some enjoyable things I might have otherwise missed. He had studied astronomy, and he monitored activities published in the newspaper. He sometimes planned for us to get out of bed at night or awaken early for a heavenly show of some sort. After we bought our RV, there was a night in Texas I remember because of that song "Deep in the Heart of Texas." It has a line about how big and bright the stars are in Texas, and as we stargazed, that tune played in my brain. When we had a hot tub placed on our back deck at the last two homes we owned, there were amazing visions in the night skies to inspire us.

Sometimes we drove to where the light pollution from civilization did not interfere with starlight. There was a marvelous night at one of the local military bases; we used Chuck's base sticker to drive onto secluded beaches at the oceanfront. I was mesmerized by the appearance of frozen ocean foam landing temporarily on the sand in cold weather. It formed patterns and then melted. Chuck inspired those quiet, thoughtful moments alone, together.

Chuck was the romantic and sexual leader in our relationship. When the movie *Dirty Dancing* came out, he wanted me to dance like the female lead, and we attempted to duplicate some of that style. I had always been the one to enjoy beach music; I liked its inspiring rhythms. We took shag dancing lessons, and sometimes I would dance with really good dancers; I seemed to be flirtatious because of those movements on the dance floor.

After Danny grew into a young man, he would sometimes go dancing with us. At one party, he acted flirtatious with me. We were being playful and having fun. Later, I realized how serious some people could be about flirtatious behavior. One sorority sister became suspicious of my behavior with the "young adult Danny" who was now "our son." Chuck was confident in my fidelity and did not get jealous over playful flirtations.

I invited my friend Cynthia to join the sorority, and she attended a Halloween party with us. She wore a black leotard and pink tutu, and called herself the Cherry Fairy. I never took her behavior seriously when she flirted with Chuck, so I was surprised when the women in our chapter wondered if she was a home-wrecker. During the secret balloting, I informed the group that I trusted Cynthia and Chuck, but not to vote her into the group if they had so many doubts about her. She was voted in, but we had not yet heard the end of this matter.

A couple inside our social group asked me if Chuck and I would like to practice swapping partners, as they did with another couple. I had never imagined we would seem to be that type of couple. I talked to Chuck about the offer, and he seemed to entertain the possibility. I explained my fears about it disrupting marital relationships, and we agreed to reject the offer. The offer had been made by one of my sorority sisters, and she put it simply, "You are rejecting us because you have that going on with Cynthia and her husband, Paul."

We vacationed with Cynthia and Paul, and Gloria and Jim, but nothing of that nature had ever been discussed or sought. Even today, I am surprised how many other people behaved differently in their marriages without my noticing.

The biggest threat to our marital relationship that I re-member happened late in our happy marriage. I was worried we would not overcome this set of circumstances. As you know, I am proud of my honesty, and I was surprised when confusion arose. In our dating life, before marriage, Chuck and I shared our sexual histories and I was totally honest, as he also seemed to be. Chuck's mom had said, if he ever made a woman pregnant, he should marry her; therefore, Chuck resisted all possibilities of intercourse, except for the one time he had reported to me. He had double-dated with a friend, and his date was a mature woman who had been married before. She made him feel welcome and safe to engage in sexual relations.

I told him my story about being a virgin until the very end of college when I fell hard for a law student who I thought loved me. I decided he was "the one," so I went to his apartment and told him I was ready to give up my virginity. He attempted to make love to me and apparently was not able to do so. I tried to get him to say he loved me. He would not commit to that, and I felt that I may have made a mistake. The next night, I saw his car in front of the girls' dorm next to ours. I knew what that meant, and I was devastated.

I tried to get a girlfriend to console me because I was certain she was the only girl I knew who was sexually active. She said that she was sorry for me, but certainly had never had sex. I was so ashamed of what I had done. I cried for a couple of days and later, when I had a date with a guy I liked, I tried to blame my resistance to intercourse on my period.

Chuck knew I dated after that loss of self-respect, without ever having intercourse again because I wanted to restore my self-control and self-worth. I felt Chuck and I were equal in our values and behavior when we got married, because we both had resisted most sexual temptations and feared an unwanted pregnancy.

Our marital crisis was when Chuck referred to our shared history and made a mistake in recalling what I had told him. In my usual dedication to honesty, I corrected him by referring to the complete story I had presented. I emphasized how similar we were. Chuck felt he should have had more sexual experience, and he liked to explore more sexual secondhand experience than I did. He enjoyed his *Playboy* subscription, going to topless bars with the guys, and some online activities that I did not notice. Maybe he would have agreed to partner swapping, but I did not want sex outside the committed relationship of love that we had.

In our intimate history, at the end of his life, I developed a better understanding of his desire to explore different sexual forms of expression. I was very content with our intimacy, affection, and sexual life. He may have taken my occasional lack of interest as a sign that he was not a good lover. That never occurred to me.

We had an amazingly good marriage, and I foolishly thought most married couples had something similar. The marriage counseling cases in my office or couples' groups were a more accurate picture of the norm. Various versions of what couples call "love" or a "happy marriage" seemed common; yet all very different from what Chuck and I had for forty-five years.

Chapter 6

Discovering the Depths

How do I begin to present the complexity of our family life? With each event seemingly handled with thoughtfulness and some respect for individuality. However, there's always some bit of personal preference or guidance, different from loved one's perspective, that creeps in. Fraught with our personal emotions and history, it can be very difficult to interpret.

Fortunately, I have told you, my reader, something about this cast of characters along the way. It's easiest to begin with Laura, my only remaining member of the original family. Let's start when she was in her teens. We had a family session because Laura stole earrings at the local store and was caught. I had carefully selected the same family therapist whom Chuck and I had seen for some marital counseling. He was very astute and well educated.

In the middle of the session, he said, "So what did your grandfather do?" Maybe I was distracted, numb, or not fully listening, but that seemed way out of context for me.

Laura proceeded as if she fully understood. The story of my stepfather, Mom's new husband, molesting her came out. We learned that Mom and this man had a habit of having the children entertain them with dancing in the evening when visiting their home. Laura developed sexually very early, but was innocent in her self-awareness. She was a very talented dancer and loved to play with her cousin when they both visited Mom. I did not know Mom had begun to join her spouse in his drinking habits, so there were no responsible adults on the scene. The picture I imagined was all of them falling onto a bed together. Apparently, Mother had Bob move the children to their own beds later, after everyone settled down.

Laura reported that she saw his penis exposed and pretended to be asleep. We, in the family session, did not hear more, but at the end of the session, we were told we would discuss what to do the following week.

I knew the choice of what to do would be given to Laura, but I felt driven to call Social Services immediately to report the incident. They found her report reliable and asked her about pressing charges in court. She did not want to risk hurting her grandmother that badly.

I realized how difficult and unpleasant it would be for Laura, but I reassured her that we could follow through if she wanted to. She still said she was unwilling.

I next called my stepfather and confronted him with the details that were reported. On the phone, he said he would ruin me if I caused him any damage. I responded that he could not ruin me because I had a good reputation publicly and privately. I was amazed at the strength of my statement and the spontaneity that I showed. I was angry and defending my daughter.

Over the next several years, my mom tried to heal from, or hide, these issues; and we constantly refused any contact. You know the rest of the story from a prior chapter. Eventually, Mom's husband wrote me a card in which he apologized for any harm he might have caused me. I told him he owed Laura his apology. He said that he could not do that because his lawyer said he could be arrested and jailed if he admitted his errors.

My relationship with my mom was very tense during the rest of her married life. They lived in assisted living as they grew older and less healthy. After her husband, Bob, died, I attempted to be more loving and supportive. At times, I was severely lacking in compassion, but at other times, I developed strategies to give her support. When Chuck and I became snowbirds, traveling to and from Florida in an RV, I found a retired nurse to take her on outings. The duty of loving a close family member stirred inside of me, but honestly, I did not feel loving. I missed the genuineness of my dad's love.

After her wedding, Laura had so little need to connect with my mom. Mom had assumed her usual role of wedding planner when Laura was married at the base chapel in Norfolk. If that began to heal their relationship, it was not apparent once Laura found a powerful new maternal figure in her husband Jim's mom. They all lived in a trailer park nearby.

Laura had chosen not to go to college, but went to business school instead. She worked at several places with loyalty and competence. She really found her special work when she decided to become a massage therapist. The chiropractor she started with was very appreciative of her abilities.

Jim, a Navy chief, was a strong partner for her. They were complementary since she was less mature, and he had been the man of the house too early in his own life. Since his father and mother had divorced and then his stepfather died, Laura and Jim were very close to his family as he was still acting as head of it.

First, I noticed Jim's mom was possibly drug dependent from medical situations. Laura learned to set limits as time went on. The biggest issue for Jim and Laura, after they married, was Jim's younger brother and his wife. Laura became extremely close to the brother's wife and, consequently, their children. That family had a crisis, and the children came to live with Laura and Jim. These events are so complex that I will wrap up with some observations.

Laura took care of three children older than her own son. Jim was away at sea a great deal, and Laura's mother-in-law was an adult who needed care.

When Jim's brother and wife reclaimed their own children much later, they criticized how their children had been cared for. I was so irritated by all of this that I almost failed to tell my daughter what a good job she had done.

In this family narrative, I will speak next of our foster son, rather than of our son, Michael. Though we had an exceptionally difficult time with Danny, Michael's story was worse.

When Danny first came to us, he would turn eighteen in March of his senior year and could not receive support from public funds unless he remained with a sponsoring family. When the worker told me Danny was a painter, I thought he was an artist, and this seemed a perfect match. Chuck and I talked this over with the children that same night, and all of us were in agreement to make the commitment.

When Danny arrived, he had his own room and we explained a little about who we were and welcomed him. The social worker had warned me the only problem Danny had was a relationship with a girlfriend. I remember saying the words that came back to haunt me many times—"No problem." I did not meet Trish, the girlfriend, before they drove to North Carolina to be married.

Danny and Trisha lived upstairs from Danny's parents after they were married. Since Danny had usually been placed in foster care as a result of his family's chaotic alcoholism, the young couple was negatively influenced by the situation. They returned in a short time; Trish to her loving mother's arms, and Danny back to us.

Chuck and I were no longer able to receive monetary support through foster care because Danny had broken the rules of his contract with the program. Danny had to be our son by personal choice. Fortunately, he had his own car with brand-new tires. I had purchased those tires, unknowing they were needed for their marriage trip. Danny was working and earning an income. He would not be a financial burden on us. I only felt the hardship of finances when he shopped for a senior ring at Kempsville High School. We were so happy he could graduate that we covered the cost of the ring and the new tires for the car.

We gave little thought to all these practical issues because we already loved Danny to some degree, and this was such a real-life drama. When I was researching his attendance record, I learned that he had not missed too many classes to graduate because the recordkeepers had too many errors in their accounting. It seemed fate was on our side. Absences from different classes varied, but he believed he could have the near-perfect attendance required for the rest of the year and still meet graduation requirements.

I was the support person for Danny's senior English theme. Unfortunately, I had made a D because Danny only brought me ten reference cards for writing "my" theme. I was lucky to earn a D since the teacher had helped Danny decide to write about her favorite subject, the Crusades. I knew little about this subject, and I imagine she may have known I wrote the paper for him.

Chuck learned helpful things about woodworking in the nighttime class Danny attended. Danny and Chuck made several things in this evening class; this was one of the many side benefits to having a talented foster son living with us. Chuck's talents did not normally lie in the same direction as Danny's, and they were good together. Our houses in Virginia Beach and Chesapeake had porches created by these two men.

Danny's friends were frequent visitors who were also welcomed in our home. Buddy helped Danny pass government, while Gary was his closest friend and coworker on many jobs. Steve was the friend who sometimes consulted on relationships, but had one failed marriage and a son already. Sometimes the guys let me in on their conversations, and sometimes they were in our personal space in very personal ways. Once, Gary's mom called to tell me that her son had brought a girlfriend for a sleepover, and precautions needed to be taken.

Danny had great time management and did house painting during some daytime and school hours. Though I was disappointed he wasn't an artist, I was pleased he could begin to make a living with these skills inherited from his father.

After Danny married Tina, his second wife, his father asked him to change his name. He was Danny Freeman when we met him, but his last name became Kepley through a court action. Danny's father said he had previously denied fathering Danny, but he was "only kidding." He stated that he always knew he was Danny's father. All of these events seemed strange to Chuck and me. We were being exposed to a side of life with which we had no experience.

As I share these stories, you may get an impression of the young man we continued to parent. He had a very difficult life with a dysfunctional family of alcoholics. We often heard stories that Danny enjoyed telling about his outrageous family. He laughed at things that sounded very painful to me.

Among these stories are instances of driving his drunken dad to work when he was barely old enough to see over the steering wheel. On one job, his dad told about adding an extra zero to the amount of a check and going to jail for his illegal behavior.

According to another story, his father was particularly proud of removing shingles from the back of the roof of a house, and doing an excellent job of installing these same shingles on the front. Later, he took the owner to admire the work in the front of the house. When the owner finally noticed the missing shingles on the back of the roof remains a mystery.

Danny had several siblings. When I met the oldest, Libby, she had been in foster care with Tina's family. The Trainos were well known to Foster Care Services since they had cared for many of Danny's family over the years. Once, I had to accompany Gary and Danny to a meeting with Ms. Traino because the guys had dated two young foster girls in their home. The dating activities were an issue, and the guys were to take responsibility for what occurred. I was overseer of more young men than I wanted to be.

Apparently, the Kepley parents had always been able to recover their youngest children from Social Services more quickly. The most amazing thing I learned about the them was the history of the family's informal "adoptions." Several children were given away to neighbors without any formal paperwork. One child became a professor at a North Carolina College. She came to meet Danny's family once, but never maintained contact. Another girl became a hairdresser and operated a local beauty shop. Danny had some contact with her for a brief period, but they did not become close. One sister could never be located. In addition to these questionable relationships, many cousins or less known relatives had dubious parentage or confusing relationships.

Danny stayed connected with us. and we were very committed to loving him. Though it was easy to love Danny, he brought many human connections along with him. I have mentioned Buddy, Steve, and Gary, who were frequent visitors to our home. The few females who visited were less frequent. Janet only stayed a few days, but we really welcomed her. She was an old flame of Danny's, and we liked her much more than Trish. Kelley was a more frequent visitor for a short period, and I hoped she might replace Trish. Even as Trish divorced Danny and had an abortion, he was hopelessly entwined with her.

Danny's wedding to Tina brought us some peace since they had two beautiful, sweet little girls, and the marriage lasted several years. Ronda captured his attention after he had been married to Tina many years. This was another blonde, like Trish, who seemed lovable and vulnerable. Ronda was on the job as a painter. She had two precious little boys, and Danny credited her for being a great mom.

It is apparent to me now that Tina seemed strong and competent as a homemaker and mother, and Ronda seemed to need help as a hardworking single woman. After Danny fell in love with Ronda, he came to see me and explained his feelings. I did not agree, but attempted to minimize my discontent. I only asked Danny to continue his strong connection with his daughters, and he promised he would.

Ronda was likable and pleasant in the beginning, and I became closer to her. I believe she became sexually discontent when Danny drank so much; she only smoked pot. I objected to the children being exposed to her illegal smoking, but Danny swore the children did not know. By the end, I only heard secondhand stories. These were dreadful stories about the children's unhappiness, dysfunction in the family, and Ronda's increasingly out-of-control lifestyle. Danny quietly began to do even more drinking to kill his pain.

When Ronda and Danny had his first son, they were devoted to the little boy. Ronda's two other sons remained close to Danny. We did not see much of the family, and eventually Tina's two girls were living outside of the home.

Going through the family chaos at this time produced unhappiness for my "granddaughters." After the newest child, Jesse, was added to the family of two boys and two girls, we became more distant from Danny's family. We had begun our RV travel and were away from home much of the time. It was many years later that I learned some of the consequences that evolved from this time of dysfunction.

Today, I call these young women my "grandgirls." You will hear more about them after they finish college and become strong and independent. All of us continue to move forward toward our better choices.

The final stories in this section of the book are about Michael, the older child Chuck and I birthed and parented. In my way of understanding, Michael's great unhappiness occurred his first year in college. He apparently had fallen in love with a young man named Michael, from North Carolina, during the summer after high school graduation.

From ages fifteen to eighteen I had arranged for Michael to have counseling regarding his questions about being gay. Both counselors agreed that he was deciding by himself but was uncertain. Chuck and I discussed this, and we had different responses. While I traced Michael's experience in the world and decided he had been stereotyped as softer and less aggressively male, I believed he was more inclined to love both boys and girls and could become sexual with either. He had only dated girls publicly, but there was much I did not know.

Over many years, I learned more of Mike's personal history and focused on his being anally raped when he was in a boys' choir during fifth grade. This trauma was perpetrated by a charismatic man who recruited the boys for the choir.

I had to put the pieces together since Michael was told by the abuser that he would kill his family if he ever told. Michael had hidden this event from all of us and had repressed the memory for most of his life.

Chuck placed more importance on Michael being less competent in sports, less interested in scouting and other male-dominant activities. Mike became interested in theater in junior high, and all these activities were frequently stereotyped as gay-male interests.

While I knew I could not do Mike's healing or the counseling that was needed, I did ask him one time to tell me about the episode of the rape. I had some training in this type of work and I was able to discern when Mike began as the little fifth grader who was injured, then became the abuser being gratified. I was aware when in the retelling his feelings changed, and I wondered if he could ever abuse children.

As I carefully reviewed my own memories, I remembered him coming home from school in fifth grade with residue in his underwear. I was convinced he had been upset because he had an accident with his bowels. I later read one of my psychology books and found that boys can begin to soil themselves if they are angry at their mothers and don't express it. I decided to examine my own behavior and ignore the accident.

I regretfully remembered his fifth-grade teacher blaming me for making him angry that year. She and I had some confrontations about whether I was making him angry at home, or she was at school. We both could have solved the mystery had we known that Michael had been painfully abused and silenced.

Both Chuck and I could accept Mike's sexual identity; however, I did not believe Michael was homosexual, but Chuck did. As a couple, we argued about Michael moving off college campus to live with his lover. The school had raised some issues about the two guys living together, and Chuck had allowed Michael to move off campus.

The importance of all this remains clear to me today. Michael told me later that he said to his lover from North Carolina, "You were dating a girl you seemed to love. If you can be heterosexual, return to her. This is a hard life."

He did not want to be gay? Was he?

As a mature male, Michael later told me that Dad Bennett had discerned his sexual orientation and said, "It's a tough life out there." Mom Bennett died before Michael's sexuality was established; she never suspected, even though Ferrum College was near their home in Roanoke, and Michael visited them frequently.

Chapter 7

Discovering Freedom

With our children mostly grown and independent, Chuck and I returned to our initial devotion to each other. We had made a commitment in the beginning we would put our relationship first, since it would be our longest-lasting investment. Because Chuck had such stable and reliable parents, we always took one week a year for ourselves, and they kept the children. We were so fortunate in this way. For years, we had an RV in which we traveled across the country, viewing interesting sites, with and without the children.

Another beautiful thing about our marriage was the fact we interacted independently for our mutual enjoyment. We sometimes chose separate activities, but usually went together. I remember one time Chuck heard men complaining about their wives going shopping; he said, "My wife doesn't like to shop." That wasn't exactly true, but I did not like to join other women for the purpose of buying something. Buying was not a recreational activity for me.

Our first trip outside of the United States was a visit to England and the British Isles. We chose there because English was spoken in both and we thought unknown foreign language might negatively impact our experience. When we arrived at the travel agency we had selected, the beautiful posters distracted me. I began to comment on first one, then another.

Chuck noticed and said, "Do you want to go somewhere else?"

Ultimately, after much discussion, we chose Greece. Neither of us had ever thought of going to Greece, but we had always liked to read about or study ancient cultures. We both enjoyed visiting the western part of our country and Mexico, where Indian cultures were represented in the ancient structures, or ruins.

The travel agency planned our trip to Greece. As novice travelers, we liked that. We went to Athens and the Greek Isles. There are so many special memories from that trip, and Santorini was our favorite stop. Athens, of course, was the outstanding experience as we saw an outdoor light show on the Parthenon at night.

When we were to return home, Kennedy Airport was shut down for international flights due to a horrendous storm threatening the East Coast. I remember my friend Cynthia said, "Poor you! You can't come home for your daughter because you must stay in Greece a couple more days!" Laura was sixteen at the time and staying with our longtime best friends, Cynthia and Paul.

A major part of returning to being and acting as a couple included special long-term friendships. Gloria and Jim and Cynthia and Paul were our closest friends. We three couples sometimes went to our time-share in North Carolina. All of us liked the same things—dining out, laughing, playing bridge, and golfing.

At that stage of our lives, the women also could do getaways, leaving our spouses to handle the home fronts. Gloria and Jim only had one son, and Cynthia and Paul had two boys about the same ages as our one-boy, one-girl family. The children could be independent with some degree of supervision.

Life was really very good, and we had mostly happy social lives. The beginning of challenges with older children was interspersed with these events. Maybe our children in their teenage years were easier to let go of since we parents had so little control as they matured. We loved them and watched them ignore our warnings and suggestions.

The most challenging events for us were the situations dealing with counseling sessions or interventions. We had help and did the best we could. Laura had dating and sexual challenges, as well as a medical problem of significance that needed ongoing treatment.

Michael was diagnosed with HIV in his first year of college and sought treatment with meds to avoid AIDS. His drug addiction began at that time since he believed he was going to die early from this disease. Michael's personal life alternated between terrible gay relationships, drug addiction, medication, treatment issues, periods of incarceration, and some purposefulness. He wanted to be a therapist, like me, and he almost completed college several times.

Breaking away from home and exploring new territory helped restore Chuck's and my mental health. From our first trip to Greece in 1984 until Chuck's death, we had about twenty years of precious connection. We traveled through Italy; we visited Mexico several times; and a favorite was a trip to Australia, New Zealand, and Bali.

When our niece was in Belgium, we flew over, rented a car, and spent an extended period visiting the British Isles. This was the first of our independently planned travel. We had planned to be hosted and assisted by our niece's family, but they received a transfer back to the US; so, they sent us instructions to use visitors' centers for any help we needed.

Of all the unusual experiences, the one in France is the most vivid. The visitors' center made reservations for us at an inn in the historic section. When Chuck saw the wooden board that was to be our chained trundle bed, he almost insisted we leave. I persuaded him to stay for just one night. I guess we were tired; we actually slept.

All of these experiences were during Chuck's retirement years, when he was from fifty-five to sixty-nine. As a civil servant in government, Chuck could retire after twenty-five years; he was fifty-five with a decent income and our home fully paid off. That allowed us to enjoy the best of leisure choices. We had saved and planned for his years of retirement. He was ready, and I was surprised he did not want to return to any work-related activities. He had an introverted side to his personality and could entertain himself well for long periods.

I was the extrovert, and even though Chuck was more introverted, our home had always been a gathering place. That was my mom and dad's influence; even though they had mostly church friends to socialize with, my mom loved to cook and entertain. My dad's personality was as an entertainer since he was attentive, engaging, and humorous. They were quite the model as they matured and dad no longer drank. Chuck and I were like them in only the best ways.

Chuck and I had New Year's Eve parties, gatherings for bridge, and celebrations of every kind. The entire blended families of our son-in-law, our foster son, and various others joined us from time to time.

Cynthia was my best friend of over thirty years. That made Chuck and her husband, Paul, seem very close. They were our closest friends in bridge playing, competitive games, similar work environments with the government, vacations, and family life. But vast differences began to appear after about twelve years.

I began my new career at age forty-two in 1979; Chuck retired in 1988. There were many years for Cynthia and me to enjoy our new professions. She received her RN soon after I began at Catholic Family Services. Both of us started out as schoolteachers and had two children. As stay-at-home moms while our children were young, we were in Beta Sigma Phi business sorority, arts and crafts, market-research jobs, and various activities together. She truly inspired me since we both liked innovative activities.

One of our best group activities was making a film, *The Perils of Purpose*, for the sorority's statewide convention. She was Snidely Whiplash, and I narrated the film; we created the plot together. We went to a restaurant called Victoria Station to tie Purpose, our heroine, to the railroad tracks. Snidely ties up the heroine in the original silent movie, *The Perils of Pauline*. Cynthia looked really impressive, playing Snidely with her pencil-thin mustache and male attire.

As I continue to examine my discovered life, I feel that Cynthia and I discovered each other in a very satisfying way. Cynthia became a responsible, talented RN while I became a social worker. No one could imagine the path we had before us.

As I worked in my new job, I learned about multiple personality disorder (MPD) from our psychiatrist. I liked Dr. David Rosen, but thought he was a little off-center. One of my colleagues shared a case with him, and I was to see this client for her regular session while he was on vacation. I said I would see her, but not honor the diagnosis since I did not believe in MPD. We agreed she would not want to talk to me about her deeper therapy, as she revealed her dissociated identities only to her regular therapist.

Later, I began to believe in MPD when I had a case in my practice. I discussed my fascination with this complicated case, in general terms, with Cynthia. A few months later, she asked for a counseling referral and I gave her the name of a coworker in my hospital practice. Cynthia was having trouble with her younger son, Stephen, and went to see Tom, the therapist, to resolve some of the difficulties.

Imagine my surprise when Cynthia told me she had multiple personality disorder. By that time, we had been friends for about fourteen years and I believed that we knew each other intimately. I decided she must want my attention very badly to make up such a wild story. I listened half-heartedly with sad disbelief until she began to fill in the gaps with stories about her respected father being her abuser. She admired her father, and his art hung all over the walls of her house. He was a college professor. Her mother, the devoted Girl Scouts leader, was an avid reader and spent time ignoring these family issues while she read book after book.

The entire story was unbelievable...until it wasn't.

My professional work became tied to my closest friendship. This may have been an opportunity for a giant leap in learning, but it put great stress on our relationship. Treating dissociation, the strongest of denial systems, can be tricky since blocked memories may be revealed. These have been repressed because the emotional and physical realities were too painful.

If Cynthia had not had a highly qualified therapist, I couldn't have gone through this with her. She shared the names of her alters with me and told me their functions. We had one instance in which I was accused of being paternal towards her. She broke contact for about six months, and I thought I had lost my best friend.

This kind of work was to be part of my specialty as I began my new career. When I finished my supervised practice at Catholic Family Services, I had a part-time hospital practice with Dr. Rosen's group and an EAP (employee assistance program) at a local Ford dealership. I took many cases with me as I began my new licensed clinical social worker (LCSW) practice at Multi-Modal Therapy. My new boss was very happy to have me bringing in additional business; we signed a contract in which I received forty percent of the income I generated when I saw some of his clients.

I only stayed there a short while since some of his business practices seemed less than honorable to me. I found a new practice base at Wellspring in Virginia Beach. I was very happy there, and I initiated many new endeavors, like a survivors' support group for those sexually abused. We also held groups modeled after AA, but dealing with issues involving children and codependency. I had always enjoyed group practice and had a separate license for this work.

At Wellspring, I was influenced by other good therapists and exposed to many new ideas. I had not heard of Edgar Cayce's A.R.E. (Association for Research and Enlightenment) or reincarnation, which several of my colleagues had studied. Our therapists' dream group was ongoing for years and extremely helpful in my self-exploration, which usually caused disruption in my church affiliations. I always moved away from traditional beliefs and went towards challenging anything with which I did not agree. The time at Wellspring became a period for deeply questioning new thoughts that had never been presented to me. During that time, I also found the Unity Church with which I fell in love.

This time, the call to something new was fraught with doubts. Most of the therapists influenced my thinking about reincarnation and past lives because they had connected with the A.R.E. Edgar Cayce was celebrated as the Sleeping Prophet because he gave psychic readings for spiritual guidance while he was in a trance. Working with dissociation and training in hypnosis left me uncertain regarding life experiences that had meanings translated into dreams or realities. All of this affected my moral conscience and religious beliefs.

An inspirational figure in our practice was Carol Bush, LCSW, who practiced guided meditations with music. Two other therapists followed her work with great respect. I sampled some of these newer ideas, but stayed true to my own therapy practice as I was graciously accepted into this office through a connection with the local clinical society of LCSWs.

I was very thankful to be joining a new group. Multi-Modal Therapy wanted me to sign a new contract so, I read it and consulted a lawyer. My boss wanted a noncompete clause and a share of the business I generated. I refused and became uncomfortable with that practice.

At Wellspring, it was a joy to work with women who respected each other. Our only male colleague moved on, and we expanded. Eventually, I brought in a new practitioner from my church. Tom Baker was a former Catholic priest who was becoming an LCSW. I offered to supervise him since I, too, had gone to Norfolk State University, where he was enrolled.

I remember the day I saw Tom at church and proposed our supervisory relationship. I returned to my seat next to my husband saying, "What have I done? I offered to supervise Tom Baker!!"

Chuck calmly said, "You are well qualified…What's the problem?"

I immediately told him of my self-doubt. Tom and I had a unique relationship.

I first learned that the school disapproved of our arrangement for his clinical practice, but their objections were overruled by his campus supervisor. I secured a business license for our practice so that Tom could receive "love offerings" from clients who wanted to pay for his services.

Working with Tom was interesting. Since I had been a devoted Baptist in my youth, and he had been a priest, we had much to discuss within our practice setting. We also both attended a Unity church, so we shared some similar beliefs. We were spiritual, but not religious. Once or twice I asked Tom to not use his particular beliefs in counseling if he wanted to become an LCSW. We had to satisfy insurance requirements, which emphasized the importance of citing medical conditions as they could be documented with specific symptoms. Our spiritual beliefs could sometimes transcend physical symptoms, but the specific symptoms needed to be validated for insurance coverage of certain mental health diagnoses. We were doing business, and there were rules that must be followed if we wanted the insurance to pay.

Becoming a LCSW requires two years of supervised practice, and I was pleased to assist Tom in his credentialing process. He fit into our all-female practice well, except for the times we mature women felt overheated; then there were slight disputes about the thermostat.

My work at Wellspring eventually led to my home-based practice. I got certain tax advantages and could be more flexible in my own space. Chuck decided to give me the garage for my private practice, and a friend helped me convert it as needed.

I was suspicious that Chuck did not want to be the home handyman any longer. He was nearing retirement and liked to travel and just be leisurely in his free time. So, I needed a handyman and Danny, our foster son, had grown into this function for us, and other people. I usually paid for his services since this was his professional career and salary.

Since I had entered professional life later than Chuck, I was eager to make a good income. I could enjoy my work while adding to our leisure fund. I remember Chuck and me doing one couples' workshop in which a man asked me, "Did I hear you say 'my' money?"

I enjoyed responding that Chuck and I had planned a traditional, breadwinner-homemaker marriage until the children were older. Then, I could be a professional worker and use my money for fun stuff. Chuck and I could point to the ways we had progressed into a long-term, satisfying marriage.

When Chuck was fully retired, he wanted to move to Florida. He had always complained of SAD (seasonal affective disorder) and wanted lots of sun and warmth to cure it. I was stressed; I wanted both his happiness and mine.

I agreed to visit Florida as snowbirds did, staying three to six months to enjoy tourist season. I went for three months and told my clients I would be away, but could come back for a short visit and catch up with them if they were managing well. Surprisingly, most people agreed they could maintain the progress they had made and would call for a telephone session (unpaid and uninsured) if needed.

The opportunity to buy a trailer in Florida arose, and Chuck asked about the investment. I informed him we could afford this more easily than continuing to maintain our RV and its travel costs, but only if the neighbor would accept a payment plan. This allowed our closest neighbors to move in together; a widow neighbor stayed in her home, and a widower joined her there.

Everyone was happy, but I still felt some stress over abandoning my spouse for extended periods. Chuck never had to leave me for long periods during his professional career, and I was making this choice of longer separations. There was some guilt, so I made a plan with him.

Chuck was close to our Unity minister in Florida, and our friend Helen loved to sing with him. I lined up a massage therapist for him, and Chuck seemed content that he would be okay while I was away. Our mutual needs were met.

While I was gone, Chuck played golf and worked for Habitat for Humanity on some homebuilding projects at church. He also sang at two places, the Unity church and the traditional church that was held in our community, Alligator Park in Punta Gorda, Florida.

Though our friends, Cynthia and Paul, moved to Florida permanently and lived in a large, beautiful new home, we enjoyed the snowbird life. We saw our children grow up. We met Danny's new family as it grew and changed. We watched Michael pursue his new identity as a gay man who was publicly out.

Michael was the saddest part for me; Chuck did better with him. I learned Michael had been sexually molested several times and had decided he was gay. Therefore, he accepted this identity and suffered the loss of partners and friends throughout the AIDS crisis. His was a very difficult life, and he continued his drug addiction and episodes of incarceration in Virginia jails. He was told, both at school and in his social world, he couldn't become a successful social worker, be active in the military, or have a satisfying partnership, like marriage. Michael spent several years on his business degree and owed many student loans when he died.

Chuck died in 2007, Michael followed him in 2015. Chuck's impending death became obvious at the very end; therefore, we had a gentle parting. The four years of treatment for non-Hodgkin's lymphoma were hopeful, until his doctor said, "I can't keep killing this man." The cancer drugs were no longer working, and they were shortening his life. The doctor was in tears when he said this to me.

When I repeated those words to Chuck, he gave up on cures or progress and began to prepare in his own way for his death. Chuck did not believe in spiritual healing, but his support groups usually did. All of us tried to advise and comfort him. I honored his own thoughts and wishes, and we had some sad and beautiful moments. He did not want hospice, but on the last day, I called them in when he was no longer coherent. I did not know it was the last day, and his special lady friend from choir, Kathy, came over and sent me out to the porch.

I had a last word with Chuck before she arrived. I asked, "You are seeing something, aren't you?"

He had a smile I can only describe as beatific, and I was reassured that he was being met by loved ones who had already crossed over. Kathy told him she would make sure I was okay and that he could leave if he was ready. He did.

I had some immediate sadness and cried, but I felt very peaceful; he had completed his whole journey here, in a wonderful way. Though he was only sixty-nine years old, I must go on alone.

Chuck is remembered as Story Man at church because he sat in front of the podium on Sundays and read to the children. He and I did *George and Gracie* together, as well as a *Cat's Meow* show with some of our theatrical friends. He was the Scarecrow on the Yellow Brick Road and sang love songs to me in public at karaoke. I have wonderful memories.

In contrast, Michael's death was a true horror story. It was the result of many dangerous same-sex relationships; I was aware he had been making self-destructive choices. I had support in my grief and some relief from my sadness as he had recently returned home from jail and been sensitive and caring with me. Michael was fifty-one years old when he died.

I was totally alone when Laura and her husband, Jim, and son, Robert, left for Jim's new job in Alabama following Jim's military retirement. Alabama was a long way away, and I felt truly alone.

Chapter 8

Discovering Myself within the Pictures

Were you a wanted and welcomed child? I'll imagine you cooed and gurgled like an adored child, even if you weren't wanted in the beginning. Perhaps we don't know at that time.

I showed up while Mom was in the midst of birth pains. I heard that Daddy was out celebrating while Mom's two sisters comforted her as she birthed me at home. I never thought much about that, but I bet Mom did.

Mom seemed to forgive Dad for his drinking many times, until she laid down an ultimatum he finally committed to when I was fifteen years old. I loved my dad, even when he was drinking, and did not see the consequences for her. In my maturity, and with my questioning nature, I put the pieces of our reality together. I wish I had told Mom my lack of feeling loved by her was a result of many things that weren't her fault.

No; maybe I couldn't do that even now because my blaming her is something I'm still working on. I wanted to forgive her before I died. I just arrived at that much sought-after place of forgiveness, and that is my cure for who I think I need to be. Could I love her for who she was, even now?

I am ending this book with thoughts about who I want to be. My close friends tell me I will be reincarnated and get another chance. I hope I have learned enough this time to get it right in the future, if I get a second chance.

You understand now, I expected others to love me. Were you told to love yourself? I was never clearly told that. I was parented by two Baptists and the churches I attended. My churches of choice became more helpful and loving in the last years of my life. And I do love me now. I don't adore me, and some days I don't like how I show up, but it is the human love I've learned to give others. I am attempting to spread this lovingness further now; and I need to understand others to love them.

I plan to do better, and I have just begun to understand who I am by writing this book. Thank you for letting me tell you who I was.

I did not begin to truly know who I was until after both Chuck and Michael died. I needed support for who I planned to be in the future. I had a few friends, a church I loved, and work that made me feel valuable. I did not immediately miss male companionship, but I learned I was extremely vulnerable a few months later.

I met a man I had known at church; he was in a group I attended and we were asked to do leadership together. He seemed to have his eye on some other women he was dating. One night, he touched the back of my neck and the feeling went into familiar places of vulnerability. Arousal and vulnerability left me wanting something I couldn't name.

While this man showed no interest, I was fine. Once he did, I was captive to my deepest emotional and sexual feelings. My husband had been sick and unavailable during the end of his bout with cancer. I had not noticed this open wound of vulnerability because I had a great history of needs well met for the last forty-five years. After becoming a widow, this man became partner number one for me, and it lasted about two years. Was I attempting to find a replacement for what I'd had?

I can report five tries for a committed relationship; I finally gave up around Valentine's Day in 2022. I guess it took me fifteen years to let go of having another male-female relationship of sufficient value. I had never realized what I had in my marriage was so valuable. Even as a marital counselor seeing some bad marriages, I thought my kind of marriage was more available to others than it seems to be.

In restructuring my love life, I took inventory. There was little left of any worth. Friendships were best, but I was accustomed to one almost-perfect (for me) man. I was accustomed to the intimate practice of our marital fidelity and forms of love.

I was usually feeling valued at work, and my church almost made me feel God loved me. My clients valued me in their own intimate moments. But some of these missing items needed reordering. Too much had been lost; I had become numb to my reality. My house was empty, and I first sought to fill it.

I started a Monday-night group at home. I initiated topics of general interest with an emphasis on spirituality. This group had some features of intimacy in our shared thoughts and respect for one another. Partner number one became part of this after we had begun a close relationship. We had met at a similar discussion group, but this one had more similarities when we explored our spiritual beliefs and behavior. I was experiencing religious healing in this group because we also shared our differences. Sharing differences was not valued in my birth family or most churches I attended.

My new partner had been married more than once, and I asked about his past relationships. He was persuasive about his last marital partner abandoning him unfairly. He had decided she might have been gay since she was uninterested in their sexual relationship.

We had a very good sexual relationship since I wanted to believe he loved me. He had been a member of my church at one time, and had been a counselor. These two points of compatibility seemed to suggest that God had selected him for me.

After I began to pay more attention to his drinking patterns, I confronted him about staying after group to share a drink with me. Our conversations were really meaningful at those times, until the fuel from the drinking carried him away into his own altered reality. He was bitter and blamed others for his unhappiness.

I began to be concerned I was expecting too much of him; my higher expectations were based on my good marriage partnership. I attempted to be more accepting. He once told me about how much the girls he was close to in high school liked his neck massages, and I remembered that first physical touch. He knew ways to touch me that seemed loving and attentive. He seemed to know where I was vulnerable. One night I attempted to stroke his hair, and he restrained my touch.

Soon, I felt physically manipulated and confronted these issues with him. That was the beginning of the end for me since he became angry. This was not love. I knew the difference. I spent two years in this relationship because I did not remember the red flags when he drank too much. He manipulated my body without reciprocation. I had never had a romantic partner control my physical touching.

When I met partner number two at my dancing group, I was impressed with how he seemed shy. He was a good dancer, and he dipped his head down while looking up at me with shy eyes. As we were leaving the dance that first night, he asked if I would drive him to his car, which was parked farther away. I was suspicious of his intentions, but it was raining, and I agreed to this short trip in my car.

When I began to pull away from my parking spot, he planted a huge kiss directly on my mouth. I was furious and yelled, "If you ever do anything like that again, I will never speak to you for the rest of your life!"

I was surprised when he began to blubber an apology, saying, "I am sorry. I am so sorry. I will never do that again."

In my experience, most guys would say, "I thought you wanted that," or something like that.

After apologizing, he exited my car quickly. He was a strange guy, but attractive, and he seemed to respect my limits. When he called the next day to see me again, I agreed to meet him at another dance; but I wanted to go independently and meet him there.

That next night, he arrived saying he had a headache, and we spent much of the time looking for someone who might have aspirin to sell or share. By the evening's end, I once again looked favorably upon him. He walked me to my car, and I gave him signals that we could kiss. He was absolutely appropriate, and I was impressed once more.

This two-month experience, was brief. I did not believe he was a man with dissociative identity disorder (DID), since that would be too much of a coincidence. Cynthia, my best friend, had claimed this diagnosis, too. I was specializing in treating this condition in my counseling work, and it is thought to be an infrequent diagnosis. Cynthia had reported her sexual abuse, and I learned she did have DID. Number two had mentioned having Tourette's syndrome, another unusual diagnosis, but said he outgrew it. I had ignored this information since I was not on the job and he was not my patient.

You may think I am wrong about his similarity to the DID diagnosis, and I would like to agree with you; but the day he drove me to the airport to catch a plane and missed a turn, I became convinced. I pointed out his mistake. Once again, he sounded like a young boy. "Oh no… oh no…oh no!!"

I directed him back to the correct turn and with a calm voice assured him it was okay. As I thought of him as a ten-year-old boy in that moment, this made sense to the therapist in me. I did not think it was appropriate to tell him my impressions, but did think I needed to do something. Later, reluctantly, I told him he seemed dissociated at times. He asked me what that meant, and I explained a bit.

Amazingly, he said, "Well, I will just have to tell people I am dissociated. I am certainly too old to go to therapy and change now."

It was relatively easy to let go of the relationship we had. I did not know who he really was. And I was not going to do therapy in my social world.

Number three of my dating relationships was a man I met online. He was the author of a book about spiritual matters and was associated with Edgar Cayce's A.R.E., where many of my friends had connected. He was a nice-looking, mature man. It was getting more and more difficult to find dating partners as I was over the age of seventy.

Our first date was to a local, historical outdoor play. This was an unusual choice for dates with romantic partners, and the setting was almost magical as the night and location were beautiful. He was slightly aggressive in his affections for a first date, and I discouraged some of his behavior. He was eager to tell me about being an actor in historical plays and some smaller movie roles, and about his book on reincarnation. I already had some interest in this subject, but was not a person who embraced this belief.

Let this be another short story. He was attractive in a flamboyant way. At New Year's, he tried to dance a tango with me. He was not a good dancer, and the tango is a difficult, dramatic dance. We shared an interest in art. He accompanied me to church and to several of my personal activities. We went to my time-share in Daytona Beach. He was a good handyman. He did not have much to offer me, except his sleep-aboard boat. I did not trust him enough to travel away with him.

And so, our relationship lasted about six months. When I broke it off, I asked if he would be my handyman. He responded he would marry me, but he would not be my handyman. We had no future together.

By the time I met number four, I had given up hope of a compatible relationship, but liked having a dating partner. He and I spent about two years in a faithful relationship, though he broke it off several times. He was being self-protective since he knew I was not interested in living together or marriage. We traveled a bit and enjoyed our daily lives together.

When my son died around 2015, we had separated permanently and he sat with my brother at the memorial service. He knew I had met number five, my last partner, and offered me to come live with him if I needed to leave Arlington, my new home address. He was older and died while I lived there.

Number five is the last of my reports regarding my dating life. I also met him online, and he seemed to be everything any mature woman might want. In fact, I was a little intimidated by his "advertised" qualities. When I first contacted him, I learned his wife had been a psychiatrist before her death. I wrote that I did not have "all those credentials." He wrote he was not impressed with credentials; I almost fell in love in that moment. Psychiatrists were acknowledged leaders in my field.

In the beginning he realized how far away I lived, and examined that journey back and forth. I was wondering if he would pursue the possibility of a relationship and was gratified when he made plans to meet me halfway at a motel in Richmond, Virginia.

At that meeting I was underwhelmed with his appearance but pleased by his presentation. As a Harvard-trained lawyer, he had made lots of money and was living in an organized, high-end community with lots of support services. I had brought my self-published book, *Translating Jesus*, and he read the entire book that night and gave me good feedback over breakfast. Our conversations impressed me and helped me recover from my intimidation about his status. He loved opera and theater and was very bright and well educated. Those were our differences, and they seemed truly significant to me since I did not have any of those exact interests or much exposure to them. I was from a different cultural background.

In the beginning, I did not know he was an atheist, but was aware he did not share my church devotion. He told me something about his parents being religious, but he and his wife attended a Unitarian church when they went to services. I had visited Unitarian churches before. I attempted to become active in his church until the leader of the group told me members were discouraged from using the name God. I needed that name to speak my own beliefs.

As I began to respect our differences, I began to have hopes for the relationship. From the beginning, I announced I would not marry because I had health insurance and a widow-support government income from Chuck that would end. Because number five was very wealthy, and I realized his family might think that was why I had chosen to move to Arlington to live with him, I was being very careful while meeting them.

When he clearly stated that Arlington had so much more to offer than Chesapeake, I accepted his assessment. I knew I might be giving up too much as I sold my home, let go of my therapy practice, and moved. Approaching the age of eighty, these actions seemed to be what I normally would do, even if I stayed in Chesapeake.

The loss of my husband and son may have impacted my blindness about a future life. I couldn't tell what to want or expect. This had always been true of my life, but I had imagined I always had good choices ahead of me. So, this time, I imagined I could have a new therapy practice in this new area. I imagined a busy social life with exciting new people and activities. And as I explored each possibility,

I became aware my partner was just adding me to his usual life, rather than creating something new with me.

Indeed, I had good choices with partner five. We traveled to China and France. We saw *Hamilton* on Broadway. His family was accepting and included me. He had a cabin home in the Catskill Mountains of New York that we visited. Our senior-living community provided meals, house cleaning, and entertainment. It was a good life, but everyone was elderly, many using wheelchairs and walkers that were visual reminders of disabilities and reduced activity. I did not like constantly seeing this reality. People were friendly enough, but I did not fit into that environment.

My close relationship to number five was sometimes problematic for me. My spontaneous reply that helped me to decide to leave him was a surprise to me. I should have noticed sooner.

I had internalized his devotion to his two daughters and attempted to overlook my feelings of neglect. These three family members were extremely physically affectionate. I had once reached out to kiss him in front of the family, and that seemed to make him uncomfortable. He enjoyed a private sexual relationship with me, but complained we did not have enough sexual interaction.

The day I decided to leave, I said, "You are not even affectionate." I was four years too late in telling him my feelings. I wish he had noticed.

I tried not to compare him to my husband, but Chuck was affectionate to our daughter and me. We had become comfortable with public affection when it was appropriate. People admired Chuck for wearing a T-shirt that said, Still in Love after All These Years. Number five gave me none of those feelings.

I don't need to tell you the entire story of number five because I am now living a new, unpredictable future after leaving him. I believe I had a period of grief after I returned to Chesapeake, and it took almost one and a half years to feel normal again. Being happy or satisfied without male intimacy is very difficult for me. I have close contacts and loving relationships with females, but I have lost my husband, my son, and my foster son. For the first time, I was not living an adult-partnered life.

I know I am alone. I was born alone, as we all are. If you have a close, loving family, you may not notice so much. Alone, now, in the important ways, I yearn for something.

Loving myself is the most important thing for me to carefully assess. Each of us is, truly, the only one who can keep a fair score as we assess our life's work and worth. I am usually happy in my new circumstances because I am approaching self-love for the first time. I have taken my own inventory to decide if I deserve love, and based on what I did receive, the answer is yes! Some precious others loved me, so I do deserve love. Being able to love others is a comfort for me.

I know I make mistakes, and sometimes I am ashamed of my habit of inappropriately judging others, but my deathbed fear is gone. I want to believe in a loving God, so I follow that central Commandment of treating others as you would have them treat you. My small world is compassionate and peaceful. I hope you will join me here and invite others.

If my story is worthwhile, I hope you can find some inspiration from the time spent reading it. Do a self-inventory. Love yourself, and love the others who show up in your life, adding to your pleasure and peace.

How angry was I when I was being taught about the God of the Old Testament? My teachers meant well, I think. In the beginning, they were some devout church members from well-established churches. Later, the people I went to church with seemed like Jesus of the New Testament. I don't mean they were near perfect or always doing the right things, but they cared about each other and learned to care about me, my husband, and our children.

They liked to share in groups, sing folk songs about peace, and have special celebrations. Once we went to the Harmonic Convergence. We simply showed up at the right beach location. People were quietly meditating, the dolphins danced before us in the distant waters, and we danced on the sand. Moments like that are a shared experience of knowing God, the Holy Spirit, and the joint energy for good in our world. I have felt this, and I wish to create more of it. I call them Jesus people, and I like them much more than the so-called Christians whom I've met in many churches.

I believe we are living on the margins of reality today, and dipping in and out of minor PTSD (post-traumatic stress disorder) and other altered experiences. I wonder if we have any idea of the degree to which we aren't truly in the same experience as the other people present with us in body, at the same time. We imagine we are together and happy, but get terribly disappointed when we realize others are significantly different from us.

Specializing in multiple personality disorder, before it was renamed dissociative identity disorder, I have had some unique visits into another person's perceived or altered reality. I learned about dissociation when they were able to retrieve their memories. Sometimes, I used my hypnosis skills with informed consent. Joining another person's reality can be either dangerous or compassionate.

During 2024, I want to dialogue about differences, experiences, and the rational and irrational conclusions each of us makes. My mission here is to love me and to get along well with others. I seem to remember as a child, that was a grade on my report card in citizenship.

Discover your own truths. Notice how you show up in life. Respect yourself. Practice AA's third step of taking your own moral inventory. Make amends if you need to.

NOW...love your own discovered life, and attempt to love all the others whose paths you cross.

Epilogue

Written by Melissa Stine, youngest of the "grandgirls"

It has been an absolute pleasure to take part in my grandmother's journey in discovering life. She has tirelessly remained self-aware every step of the way, seeking out her own truth. Every person she meets, relationship she builds, is intentional and FULL of who she, unapologetically, is. I have zero doubts the God we know aligned the stars for my father, Danny, to be lovingly accepted into her home. Like others who have known and loved Dawn, I too, have followed in many of her footsteps. THAT is how inspiring she truly is.

As I've watched her continued growth and vigor for living an authentic life, I cannot help but look forward to the fruits of any labor she commits to put forth. As she awaited the next step in completing this book, she was in a terrible car accident that greatly impaired her ability to perform the tasks needed to conclude publishing. Even in the state of hyper-fixation and anxiety of what might come as a result, she stayed completely in tune with what God was showing and doing in her life.

It is with great confidence I say, she has officially broken free of any rule-following mold or expectations, allowing life to happen to her, versus because of her. From her vulnerable beginnings in the church, to her powerful leadership within it, she has forged her own way and set of beliefs, no matter the controversy they may cause. The healing that has occurred throughout her life to get to that point, and now even after, is a blessing to anyone who knows her.

I encourage all of her readers to really invest the love she has in others, into themselves and those around them. "Take your own inventory," as she would say, and be authentic to who you are and what you believe. Recognize your shortcomings and where you could have done things differently, while still honoring your actions as you begin living genuinely in every moment. Then, watch as life introduces people and circumstances that make life rich and full.

This will be the best investment you can make as you live and later, discover, life.

Let's Connect

Get to know Dawn Bennett!

Email: rdben865@gmail.com

Facebook: Investing Love

Previously self-published: *Translating Jesus*
(questions major religious thought)